CW01306400

# Konversations with my Kids

Building extraordinary
relationships with teenagers

Ana R. Gracia

Copyright © 2016 Ana Rodríguez

All rights reserved

Cover design: Ana Rodríguez

ISBN-13: 978-1523708956
ISBN-10: 1523708956

*For Ray, an awesome father.*

*Love,*
*Judy*
*Feb 2018*

To the true authors of this book:
my beloved children

# WHAT'S IN HERE?

WHAT'S THIS BOOK ABOUT? ..................................................... 1
1.  PETS AND LOVE ............................................................. 3
2.  THE BIG CAR ................................................................ 17
3.  STORIES ....................................................................... 40
4.  WAS I EVER A CHILD? ................................................... 57
5.  GOD! I CAN'T BELIEVE THIS! ........................................ 67
6.  WHAT WILL I BE WHEN I GROW UP? or ¿QUÉ SERÁ, SERÁ? ................................................................ 83
7.  YUMMY! ....................................................................... 98
8.  STAR WARS ................................................................. 117
9.  MONEY ........................................................................ 129

# WHAT'S THIS BOOK ABOUT?

The heroes of this book, my now 13 and 15 years old children, are happy. Simple as!

I'm sharing here with you the kind of konversations we hold together. I listen to them and learn from them. They listen to me and learn from me. We all grow.

We get to see, every day, what unconditional love is like, how fulfilling it is and how far it can take us to in every area of our lives.

**Kids:** teach your parents how you wish to be treated.

**Parents:** abandon your old stories and accompany your children in their journey to discover who they really are.

# 1. PETS AND LOVE

## Context

What is *love*? How does the emotion of love work?

I think there's no other topic in the whole world that had been addressed more often, by talking about it, writing about it, singing, filming, photographing... You name it.

Well... yes: about love and also lack of love.

This is an emotion that makes a tiny organism, that you can't even see with the naked eye, hook up with another one and generate a new life. Love makes pigs tenderly breast feed the cubs of their predators. Kings relinquish their thrones for love, towers and palaces are built up for love, kingdoms are conquered for love. Even murders are committed in the name of love.

Who talks about love? Poets, singers, scientists, enlightened people, glossy magazines, our neighbour next door and anyone who can communicate in any manner. But, do we really understand what they say? Do we really feel all this emotion of love carries along if we've never experienced it before?

Can we measure love?

Feel free to visit the *HeartMath Institute* (www.heartmath.org). Here, you can find a lot of reports with numbers, figures spit out by a machine; paradise for Descartes fans!

For other mortals that don't care so much about scientific reports and data but prefer lay man's terms, a couple of questions: when we are in love, what are we capable of? Do we smile often? Do we feel strong inside? What colour does life look like? Do we allow ourselves to dream? What speed does time move at?

Let's go a bit deeper. Take some time, look inside and review your life. In the name of love, what have you done for your children, your family, your friends, your colleges... your pets?

I know, I know... Some of the things we've done are... well, let's say we wouldn't mind forgetting them at all!

There is a movie which had a huge impact on me: *Poltergeist*. The little girl starring the film was Carole Ann. She happened to be swallowed by some entities living in a parallel realm with the gate being their television set.

The medium helping bringing Carole Ann back to this 3D reality kept telling the girl to hold on tight to the love she had for her parents and her family and that they all had for her. She kept repeating that love would make it possible for Carole Ann to come back home.

To hold on to what?? I didn't get it. Those words got tattooed in my neurones back in the 80's and I couldn't make any sense of them until the mid-noughts in the 21$^{st}$ century. It's as an adult when I feel something like a halo of special energy around those who grew up surrounded by love in their homes. In my mind's eye, I see they have very big roots, very strong foundations. As a child, I was always able to tell what other children came from troubled families.

At this stage in life, I've also learned there are different ways to communicate love and to experience it[1]. According to Gary Chapman, there are five languages: words of affirmation, quality time, receiving gifts, acts of service and physical touch.

They recognise the environment for maximum growth is in a marriage, and I mean living together under the premises of any sex combination and any legal arrangement possible. In this grounds, imagine one of the spouses speaking the receiving gifts language and the other one speaking the physical touch language; yes, you guess right: the result is the same

---

[1] *The Five Love Languages*, Gary Chapman. http://www.5lovelanguages.com/

as one person talking in English and the other one in Spanish, both of them using perfect grammar and pronouncing perfectly: just like a lizard trying to explain a fish how to sunbathe on a rock.

Children also have their preferred ways of communicate love. The more we speak their language, the more they'll perceive love and the stronger their foundations to overcome any challenges will be. For their entire life.

## Talking with Jamie one evening during Christmas holidays

— I love Egg so much! See how cutie he is! I so love him! I can't stop caressing him.

— How lucky this cat is, living with us, isn't he? We treat him so well!

— No! We are the lucky ones, because he lives here.

— That's a different perspective. I had never looked at it that way. Thank you.

— He's so round and fluffy and soft. So lovable! Look at his whiskers and the patch here. Have you seen these little hairs over here? And this black foot pad and all the others are pink? Have

— you?
— ...
— Aww! He's soOo adorable and beautiful and perfect!

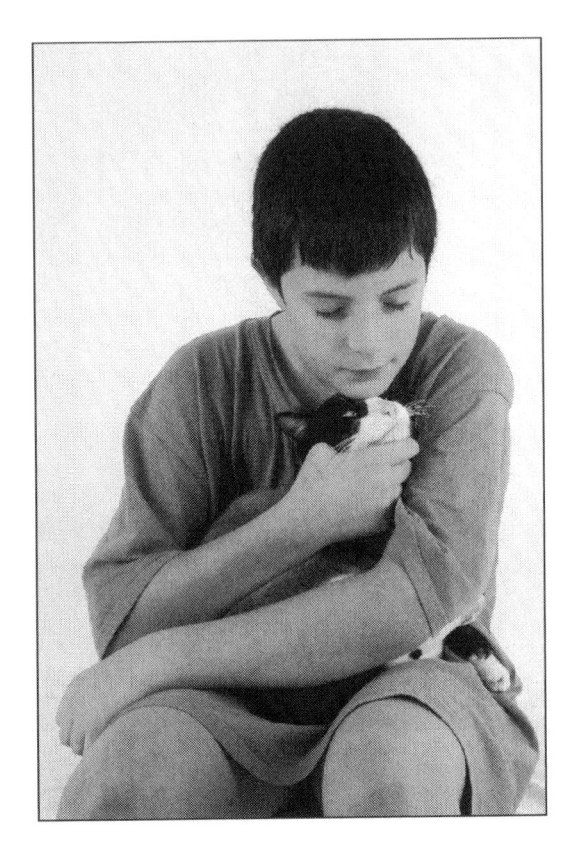

— I'm so delighted that you look so carefully at those little things mother nature produces with so much detail and care and we often take for granted or don't appreciate.
— Have you looked deeply into his eyes, how blue they are? And if you see here, look! The hairs in his ears get shorter and shorter just perfectly. And look at the hooks in his tongue. They're so weird!
— I'm guessing they happen to be very useful for cleaning himself up, with so much hair all over.

— It's a bit disgusting when they lick their ass...
— If you say so. Did you notice they, cats, seem not to notice bad smells? And I mean terrible smells.
— I know! How come they can stand the smell of another cat's arse? They stick their noses into the other's asses just like that!
— I think that's the way they recognise one another.
— That's disgusting!
— Judgement! It's disgusting for you! I'm not aware... if I ever told you... When I lived in Ireland, a friend of mine came home for dinner and we gave her boiled rice with fried eggs and tomato sauce. We call that 'rice Cuban style'. For her, that was the strangest mixture she had ever seen in her life.
— Eggs and rice? Really?
— You bet. And that happened among two European countries with not such big cultural differences between them. You know they eat insects in some places, right?
— Sure!
— And even more strange things, just like this man who wanders all over the place and eats anything he lays his hands onto... What's his name?
— Bear Grylls, the last survivor. One day, I saw him eat a spider as big as my fist.
— With hairs and all?
— Alive! And another day, he found a dead seal, all full of worms because it was rotting; he picked the worms, put them in his sock, in the very sock he was wearing, boiled everything and ate it all.
— Sock and all?
— No, mum! The inside! The worms only! The worms that were eating up the seal making it rotten, boiled in a dirty and sweaty sock.

— Sure. Only that.
— Look at Egg. He's sleeping now. He's a bit lazy, this cat. He spends so many hours a day just sleeping.
— You see the way he loves when we stroke him between the ears? He purrs so much!
— Sausage prefers we stroke him in his belly and lifts up his leg so we have full access.
— And Divi loved being scratch around her mouth. That was unique!
— And Mandie doesn't like being lifted up.
I never thought of that but you're right, they all prefer different things.
— Same with humans. Everyone wants and needs to feel love, but we all perceive it more if it comes to them in a certain way.
— What do you mean?
— You love talking and us doing things together and you hug and kiss and hold hands all the time. Your friend John likes talking about the presents he receives from his family and the biggest smiles I get from him is when I say to him that I baked a pudding especially for him.
— Mmm. I see.
— I need to feel skin in a regular basis, and hugs, and pats on the back, and touch people when I talk to them and I love it when you guys do things at home, or run errands for me with dad. And dad loves it when we say to him how good a father is, what beautiful hands and legs he has and how we appreciate all the night shifts he takes at the hospital.
— Egg likes the special canned food we get him from Santa.
— True!
— Look! He seems fully awake now because there's a bird in the garden. Look at his ears moving to the sides! He's so cute!

— One thing is clear to me, son.
— What?
— That you know perfectly what the meaning of unconditional love is.
— And that is...
— That means you love Egg no matter what. You love him because he just is.
— Of course! I also love you although you tell me off sometimes. So?
— Great! Me too. Whatever you do. I've always tried to make sure you understood that one thing is what you do or say, your behaviour, and another thing is you. You see? That message didn't always come across from my parents to me when I grew up.
— Mmm?
— As I grew up, I was told all those rules good girls were supposed to follow to get the label of 'good girl'. For instance: good girls don't shout, don't get pissed off, don't complain, would obey adults all the time, don't eat in the street, don't run like boys, would always sit down properly with their legs very close together, would dress with modesty...
— What's that?
— Never mind.
— Isn't all that a bit silly?
— I didn't know any better and they didn't know any better either. And it was the same standard for all girls. In my little world, I mean.
— Because they spanked you otherwise?
— Actually, your grandmother loved using her slipper as a spanking device, yes. But, deep down, what I discovered as an adult is that I followed all those rules so my mum would love me and everybody else would accept me.
— But granny loves you.

— Sure. But, you see, the message has a few more layers: on the one hand, we have the 'good girls' thing, they do or don't do such and such and, on the other hand, she loved telling everybody her girls were 'very good girls' and how much she loved them. So, my sister and I had to be good girls so my mum wouldn't be seen as a liar and the fact that she always added how she loved us was understood as 'if they were not this good, I wouldn't love them'. I'm not saying she wouldn't, I'm just saying how I heard it.

— Sounds difficult!

— Very twisted, I'd say. But that's what the way it was. Monkey see — monkey do: our parents just repeated what they learned from their parents, generation after generation.

— Mmm.

— I might even be a bit boring, telling you all the time how much I love you and repeating over and over that, whatever you do, I still love you. That doesn't mean I love all the things you do, but it's important for me that you can see the difference between what you do and yourself.

— No, you're not boring...

— Come on! You think I am! I've just told you the same thing twice in less than two minutes!

— See how he yawns! So pretty! Look! He's stretching out now. The nerve of him! And lies down on his other side! As if he were tired! Amazing!

— You know Egg won't be with us forever, right?

— I know. But I feel so much love for him that it compensates it all. I rather have him. It's like this thing inside and I feel it and I feel like hugging him so tight. I love him so much!

— You know what, sweetie?

— What?

— I'm so, so grateful! Do you want to know why?

— Why?

— Because I think you're experiencing Love with a capital L. The love that fills you up with energy and light. The unconditional love I just mentioned before. You already have this reference of how you feel when you're immerse in the energy of love, it is already a part of your foundations. And you can use that emotion for anything. Look: you love Egg because he is the way he is, you don't stop loving him if he doesn't do what you want him to do, if he doesn't play when you would like him to play, if your jumper ends up full of cat's hairs. It doesn't matter what he does or he doesn't, you love him the same.

— He's so cute! How couldn't I?

— Now you know the emotion. It took me years to feel it, because I was full of fear and fear is the opposite to love, because you either feel one or the other.

— Sometimes, I feel hunger or thirst.

— Ha, ha! Indisputable!

— What?

— You got me speechless. Once again!

— I'm sorry.

— Don't be sorry! I just meant there are two kind of emotions: those that make us feel good and those that make us feel bad. The emotions that make us feel good, we call that love and we call fear those making us feel bad.

— For instance?

— Think of Egg. What do you feel?

— Mmm! So cute!

— Look at yourself: you're looking up, you're smiling, your eyes are

shining, you breathe slowly; everything in your voice and your body shows love.
— I see.
— Now, think about the smashed slug we saw last weekend when we were going for a walk.
— Yuk! Disgusting! But I wasn't fearful.
— You're frowning, your body shrinks, you moved your head to the left and backwards, as if trying to get away from the slug. Would you accept you'd feel fear of being touched by it, that you'd feel bad if I took the smashed slug and I put it on your lips?
— That is yucky yuck!!!
— But you kiss Egg all the time.
— But he's cute and lovely and soft!
— It's an animal that licks his ass and then he licks you and eats mice that he's not cleaned or peeled before.
— Ahh...
— Not cleaning mice before eating them means that all the hairs go in and the pee and poo of the mice also goes through his throat.
— Yuk, yuk, yuk! You didn't need to tell me all those things!
— My point is despite the mental image you have of Egg now, you still love him.
— I see.
— Note something else: we've only imagined it all. Egg is behind you, therefore, you can't see him. And the slug, who knows where it is now. See? Think of all those reactions just by thinking; it's just thoughts, it's only in our minds, but they produce physical reactions.
— So?
— I'm guessing I'm beating around the bushes here, but there's a

connection: I was thinking that us, adults, tend to think about things over and over because we're scared of what it could happen or because we start assuming and guessing this and that and it's just tricks our minds play on us! We create it all!

—...

— I see. You can't follow me now. That's because I've had an 'a-ha' moment and failed to communicate it to you. Ok. An example. Remember that day we went to the movies, it was a very funny one and I didn't laugh at all, and you couldn't understand why?

— Yes! Everybody was laughing so hard sometimes we couldn't even hear what they said, but we still laughed even though we didn't hear the jokes.

— That day, I spent it all, no, wasted it all, thinking of a conversation I had held with a friend. In this conversation, all of a sudden, she started screaming at me and throwing things to my face, metaphorically, that I absolutely knew they were her stuff, her story, nothing to do with me. But I took it personally and it hurt so much. Then, in the movies, I was reliving the conversation, my pain, other stories that had hurt me in the past. I felt small, I breathed shallow, my body was shrunk. I felt abused, miserable... How silly of me!

— But the movie was very funny!

— Yes, love, but I chose to dwell on the pain. See? That's something you teach me all the time: you're always in the moment. You've mastered that and I learn from you.

— You learned that from me? Really?

— I do learn from you and I thank you for that.

— Wow!

— So, as you can see, our mind can't distinguish between what's outside

and what's imagined. For our mind, there's no difference. And we end up making our thoughts true.
— So... if I think of a pudding, will I find one baked in the kitchen?
— Could be. But, it'll be a lot easier to materialise one if you bake it yourself.
— Shit!
— But! If you think of a pudding and I'm very present, completely focused in this moment, I could pick your thought, think it's my idea, and go bake a pudding myself.
— Like the other day, when I was thinking of a song and you started whistling it?
— Exactly! And so many times, when one of us says something and the other says they were thinking about that just at that very moment.
— Cool.
— Yeah. It's magic. And I think that should be the normal, rather than the exceptional.
— I'll lie down there with Egg and I'm going to think very hard... that my homework gets done by itself...
— Little distinction here, son. The way it works is you think of something you wish, release it and then make sure you are in the present, very attentive to clues. You'll start getting information, things will be presented to you as if by magic. Then, it's your turn to move your ass.
— You want me to dance?
— I mean, take action. We can materialise anything we can imagine, but we need to take the necessary steps. Do you think Rafa Nadal just lies down on the sofa thinking of tennis, goes to the tournaments and just wins? No! He'll probably envision this, but sure thing he trains a lot.
— Do we make a pudding?

— Sure! A chocolate one?
— Aren't they all?
— Silly me! This pudding is going to taste wonderful.
— Why?
— Because it'll be baked with a lot of love. Anything you do with love, you can feel it with all your senses.
— Can you?
— You can!

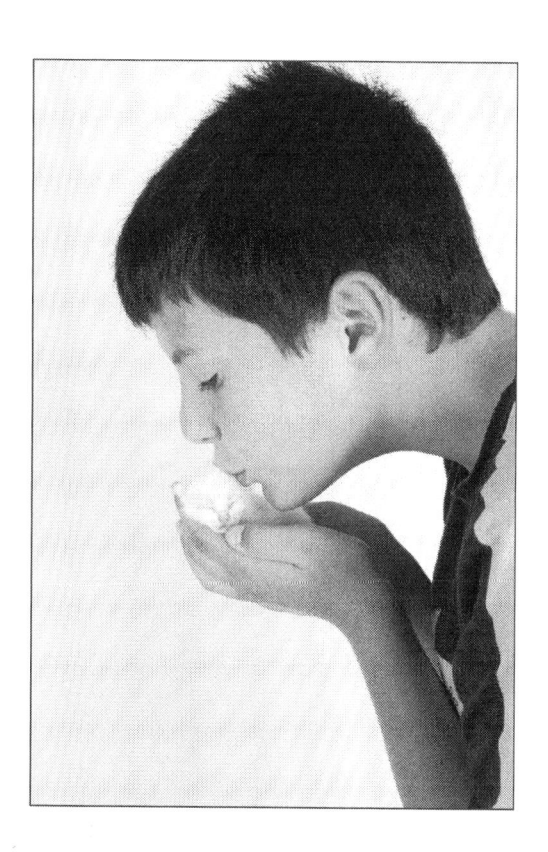

## 2. THE BIG CAR

### Context

The other day, coming back from school, the children were so joyful. At least, that's what I perceived. I felt their happiness and joy. And they felt safe as well. I know it's all filtered through my own experience, but I can easily recognise when children don't feel safe because I've been there.

This image of complete joy will live long in my memories. Along with a huge feeling of gratitude.

The part of the security thing was enhanced by the fact that I was driving my new big white car. Every time I drive it, I can feel gratitude and safety in all my cells.

For many months, more like a couple of years, I kept the photograph of my dream car where I could see it every day.

First, it was the desire for it; then, the mental image. To help with the visualisation, I went to the car dealer and asked for an offer. As soon as was at home, I cut off one of the pages of the manual, with a photograph of the car in the colour I wanted, I put it up at the fridge door.

Some days, I wouldn't even notice that the photograph was there. Other days, I looked at the picture with a bit of a sad feeling inside because it hasn't come true yet and the ghost of failure floated around me. In short: my faith was not always at its strongest. I think that was the very reason why the big white car didn't appear in the tri-dimensional realm faster. But, most of the time, I looked at the photograph and smiled imagining I was inside it, driving my children around.

<u>The why.</u>

Step number one for a dream to come true is, obviously, to define what it is that we wish.

Number two would be the reason why we want to make it happen.

In my example, the main reason was safety: I wanted the big and powerful car because of its safety features and it's my children I drive around, no less. I must say I love cars, so that was another reason. And a third one would be to show my children, by example, that if we wish something with enough intensity, we consider it done, we don't get attached to the outcome and, important, we are aware of the clues and intuitions that we receive and take action on them, then we'll be able to hold in our hands what it was first only inside of us. Or something better.

## Konversation with Jamie and Mario driving back from school

— Come on, guys! Let's drive our big white car home!
— Will you let me play Eminem?
— Of course! Bring the connection for the phone.
— So cool!
— It's so exciting!
— Pick a number from 1 to 12.
—4.
— Rap God. Good choice.
— Louder, please.
— Ok. So this is D for Direct. It's so great not to change gears!
— Na na na na na na na na rap god, rap god...
— Hold on! Let's take a picture from the outside. And we can put it up at the fridge door, together with the old one.
— Boring! Let's take it when we come back. Or another day.
— Fine. We can take it another day.
— Rap god, rap god...
— I like this musician. I must confess I had never listened to rap

songs attentively and since I didn't know anything about rap, I was pretty switched off and couldn't tell one rap singer from another; all songs sounded very much the same to me. But I can feel now that Eminem absolutely loves what he does, and that love, plus a huge amount of hours of work and looking for improvement all the time, I'm sure. What was I saying? Ah! Yes! I can feel all that passion and well done work and it makes me feel it's an extraordinary artist.

— Thanks a lot, children, for putting me in touch with a kind of music and art that was completely alien to me.

— There's a movie with him on it, and he's the actor being himself. Can we watch it?

— Of course!

— Yippee!

— I'd love you to feel appreciation for this car we're in. Whichever way you are more comfortable with. Maybe tapping into the feeling of safety because this car is more robust and powerful than the old one. Maybe because the engine is very silent and smooth. Perhaps because the music sounds a lot better and we can even plug our phones into the system. Or because it's bigger and higher than the other and we can see further. Do you remember what our financial situation was when I put the photograph of a car like this up in the fridge?

— Nope. Were we poor?

— It was a few months after I stopped receiving the dole payment. I was extremely worried in case we couldn't keep paying the fees of your school. Not being able to send you to this school was like the end of the world for me. I know now that was only my perception and we'll go back to this, because I'm beating around the bushes.

—...

— OK. See how everything was in my head: your dad and I lived in the same house, with the same amount of money. I lived in scarcity and he didn't. I couldn't think of anything else but how to get more money. And I didn't want to back to trading my time for money working for somebody because by doing that for 20 years, I grew to be very unhappy. Your school... Your school... I was obsessed with your school fees. And when I was the most worried, bang! The engine of my car breaks down.

— Did you crash?

— No, sweetheart, I didn't. It started making a funny little noise, I brought it to the garage and they told me it was broken and that I needed a new one. It was €5,000 and, at that moment, we had €6,000 in the bank. So do the math.

—1,000.

— Exactly. I had such a bad time. And thinking that many children have nothing to eat made me feel even worse, because I know your experiences and your childhood at home have a lot more an effect on your development than school. At least, I think so, but the little voice in my head kept talking and moaning and I did nothing else but repeating to myself 'I don't have enough, I don't have enough, I don't have enough...'

— Ahh.

— So, one day, I took you to the Audi car dealers. Do you remember? We went to see the car I wanted, the Q5. We got in one of the cars, felt it, smelt it and asked for a proposal. I told the dealer not to call me, that I had no means at that moment, but that I would go back to buy it.

— I remember! There were two like this one and one even bigger.

— Yes. A Q7. When we got back home, I cut out a photograph of the book with the photograph of the car and Mario added a drawing of his head, so he could envision himself in it.

— Yes! I remember that! And Jamie said it was him, but it was me.

— Sure. I wrote down the date I wished to get the car for. We passed the date and I still had no idea how I could buy it. God delays are not god denials, though. Back then, I had already

found the project that would allow me to get my dream big white car, but I couldn't see it.
— That's weird.
— Well... Do you remember what I told you about making things real, about creating the things we think about? Sometimes, we create a happier life and, some others, just the opposite.
— What a silly thing. Why would someone wish to be less happy? Hold on! This bit is just great: *Don't be a retard/be a king?/think not/why be a king/when you can be a god?*
— Wow? This Eminem is singing those words at the right time!
— Yeah!
— All those months, I used to look at the photo on the fridge and I must admit that I thought of taking it down more than once because it made me feel a failure. Do you know what failure is?
— Like when you don't pass an exam?
— And when you train to win a race and you don't win, right?
— It could be. That's what I used to think too. But I read a lot and also listened to those CD's I play in the car, remember?
— Of course. They talk and talk and never sing.
— Well, they say failure is just not having learned.
— Learning what?
— It makes sense to me that things happen so we learn from them. The way we put a label of good or bad, success or failure is just duality.
— (I don't understand anything. Do you, bro?).

—(Nope!)

— Do you know who Hellen Keller was?

— No clue. I know Keller. From *On Mice and Men?* No. It was another book I read in school about some Keller guys who sold pieces of airplanes to the US.

— I mean another Keller. Hellen. When she was younger than 2 years, she got sick and became deafblind. She could speak a bit, but she was not easy to understand because she couldn't remember the sounds.

— Wow! That's awful!

— See? That's what I meant by duality, by judging and concluding that was bad.

— Mum! It was very bad luck that she got sick and couldn't see and hear ever again!

— With the help of Ann Sullivan, Helen learned to communicate. And she did so many things for the blind community! She wrote books, and she was also involved in politics. Helen got to be friends with remarkable people of her time and even got a degree. All those things are not normally achieved by anyone, let alone a woman, let alone a deafblind woman!

—So it was good not to see and hear and speak funny?

— She chose, let me say it again, she *chose* to make the most of it. Those were her circumstances and she decided to keep going with life and, as a result, she's been an inspiration for thousands of people in the world. Everyone knows her.

— I didn't.

— Me either. I don't think the children in my class would know her.

— I'll send you a link to your WhatsApp so you can read it and share[2], if you like.

— Cool!

— So what seemed like really bad, a huge disgrace, it showed to be perfect, as so many benefit from her work and example. She still inspires people today, and has been dead for around 50 years. You can see videos of her in YouTube and she seems happy and fulfilled.

— Dead and deaf and blind. Bff!

— Now tell me another number from 1 to 12.

—7.

— Go to Sleep.

—...

— Do you understand everything he says, mum?

— Not all. But I do understand a lot of swear words.

— He, he... Lol!

— Going back to the fridge: when I looked at the bank account and then to the photograph of my dream car, I was incapable of seeing how the car was going to turn from a picture on paper into a 3D big white car parked outside. So, do you know what I used to do?

— What?

— I got into the old car and imagined it was the new big white one.

---

[2] https://en.wikipedia.org/wiki/Helen_Keller

I imagined I didn't have to change gears because the new car was automatic, I imagined I was driving a much bigger and higher car, a very powerful one. I felt the smell of new car and the softness of the wheel. When I was in bed, I visualised the two of you in the car, one in the co-pilot's seat and the other one behind, playing songs at full blast.
— Can I put the volume up now?
— Yeah, that positive thinking you always talk about.
— It's more than that. But, what did I use to do next?
— Don't know.
— Work hard!
— Ah! Ok. Yes. With the computer and talking on Skype.
— Some people out there talk about wishful thinking, which is thinking about things really hard and repeating affirmations all day long. Then, after a while, they give up and say it doesn't work. This is how it works for me: first, I think what is it that I wish, I focus on it and I imagine in my head what it would be like when that wish has already happened. And then, I'm very alert to what's going on around me and to my intuitions, because everything gets me closer to my wish. Plus one more thing, guys: once my wish is there,
visualised and felt, I completely give up on it.
— Bff! Sounds tough.
— W-what? What do you mean by give up on it?
— Yes: if I end up not getting whatever I wish, a thing or an experience or a result, I understand that's because there's

something better awaiting me or because that was not the best outcome for me.

— ...

— And, don't you think. For me, allowing myself to think big is quite challenging, because I was taught to do things differently and also that so many things were out or reach because they were the domain for the rich only, or it was not appropriate for girls, or it was bad, or it was a sin... You wouldn't believe all the crap I believed!

— A sin is...

— It's doing something bad to you or to others, according to somebody else's criteria: parent's, religion's, teacher's...

— Like drinking soda?

— More like insulting, telling lies, steal, hurt, kill. These are pretty clear. Do you feel ok after shouting names to each other? ¿Or when you hit each other when you were little? When you think you have won, perhaps you felt great for a while, but it was a lot more rewarding and fulfilling when you played together, right?

— Jamie is a bit annoying sometimes.

— Mario always wants my things.

— I was also told that it was sinful to feel clever, think that you were good at certain things, thinking about boys, have a lot of money, rest or sleep for too long, say swear words, touch oneself...

— OooOOooh!

— OooOoooh!

— In summary: what works for me is have a clear picture of what I wish. I then see it in my mind's eye and experience it with all my senses. I'm grateful because it's here already. I'm very focus in the moment to detect the clues and take action. When I'm distracted and, over all, dwelling in sad things from the past or worrying about the future, then I miss all the clues and feel crappy.
— And the old car?
— That was the best of it all! The best by far!
— Did you enjoy getting the new car at the dealer's?
— So much! But I enjoyed the part of the old car a lot more.
— Was it more fun? Did you destroy it with a hammer? And you never told us??
— No, honey. I didn't smash it with a hammer. I gave it away.
— And that was more fun than go get the new car? Really?
— One day, I met with a school mate of mine. We hadn't seen each other for many years and we were talking for like 5 hours in a row.
— Talking? Talking all the time? More than a whole football game!
— It's like more than 60 battles of World of Tanks. Holly Molly!
— We talked about many things and one of the things she told me was that she was renting a car some months.
— And why didn't she buy a new car with all the money she spent in renting?
— Something to do with her ex-husband and lawyers. She told me,

but I didn't record the details because my focus was on the fact that she was renting her car and some months that was a bit of a stretch. So what I thought there and then was: "I am going to give my friend a car. When I buy myself the Q5, I'll give her my current car".

— Did she ask you for it?

— No. Even though the circumstances in her life are improvable, she's a very joyful and positive person and just keeps going. She doesn't entertain suffering. She's such a great example.

— So what did she say when you gave her the old car?

— I called her on a Sunday evening and told her I had a present for her, would she accept it. She couldn't believe it! "Really? Are you really giving me a car? Me? Why?" So I said yes, I was giving her a car. I told her the remote control to open the doors didn't work, the co-pilot's door was a bit stiff and the thing to splash and clean the windscreen was stuck. "Does it run?" "Of course it does! We were using it until we brought home the new one" "A car! A car for me! And it works!"

— Is that the friend of yours we met yesterday in school?

— No. You don't know this one.

— And what else?

— When she came home to pick the car, she told me that as she hung up the phone after talking to me, she walked into the kitchen with her children. She was very pale and speechless. Her kids were asking her "What's wrong, mommy? Are you ok? Is daddy ok?" "Yes. I've been given a car". "A car with doors that runs?" "Yes.

All for us" "Does Moon fit into it?"

— What moon?

— Moon is a big dog they have. "Yes. Moon fits". "Can we keep it forever?" "Yes. Forever. It's a present".

— In 4 years' time, when I can drive, will you give me your Audi?

— We'll see.

— And couldn't you have sold your old car?

— Yes, I could. I could have sold it and I would have gotten some money for it. But I had this chance to make real a dream that I had. And you know what? When she sat down at the wheel, she was so excited that she forgot to press the clutch and she was all confused with the pedals!

— She couldn't drive?

— She's been driving for over 20 years. But she was so nervous and excited and thankful and grateful that, let's say, her

intelligence got a bit distracted for a split second.
— Did she turn stupid?
— She was so used to giving and so little used to receiving that she didn't know how to react. That's my hallucination, anyway. I'm guessing her body's reaction was to reject the present and that's why her body refused to drive. As I said, that's a guess.
— I love been given presents.
— And do you enjoy giving presents away?
— Yeah! That too!

— I think it's great you enjoy both giving and receiving. I was taught to give and I was also taught that giving was better than receiving, and I know now that means you're denying somebody the pleasure of giving. Nowadays, I think what they told me doesn't make sense because, if I don't receive, I would have less things to give. Even worse: when I was little, they made me give away things I wanted to have for myself and I didn't have. That frustrated me so much! That's why, when you were younger and we got your friends a present for a birthday party or something, I always offered to buy something for you too, because you're number one for me and I wanted you to see it.

— Oh. I never noticed.

— It doesn't matter. I'm sure you felt it at some level.

— Huh. Thank you... I suppose.

— Can I tell you what I learned with the new car?

— Sure. Can I play another song?

— Of course you can. Would you mind put the volume down a bit, sweet?

— I learned a lot of things. For example, I learned to accept that if I didn't get it, that was ok and there was no need for me to feel guilty or a failure. I also learned not to lose faith even when materialising it seemed to be completely out of reach. Did you ever hear *faith moves mountains*?

— Is that a song?

— Is it a movie?

— Maybe. I know this expression from the bible, from religion. It says: "[...] if you have the faith the size of a mustard seed, you will say to this mountain, 'Move from here to there', and it will move; and nothing would be impossible to you".

— What's mustard seed?

— A tiny little seed. You've seen mustard as sauce: the red bottle is tomato and the yellowish one is mustard. They offer them in

places with hamburgers and chips.
— Yeah. It smells funny.
— So we can move the Everest and bring it right here? That would be so cool!
— I think it's a metaphor. I think it means that if we can manage to hold something in our mind with absolute certainty, without wavering, we could get anything we wished even though what's in front of us now and what others might say around us show a different picture.
— That's like the Tony Robbins' thing of walking on fire.
— Exactly! Experience tells us fire burns and that if we get very close to something hot, we get burnt.
— Like that day when I put my finger in the stove and it hurt very much and you put a leaf around my finger and it still hurt at night.
— That's it: you got too close to the stove and you burnt your finger.
— No. He actually touched it. So dumb!
— When wood burns, it gets very hot and anything we put in the stove burns as well. When we place potatoes wrapped up in tin foil, they get cooked.
— And if it falls or gets torn, they get black and taste awful.
— However, when we walked on fire, none of us got burned. And they were really hot!
— They added more when it was my turn!
— If we had put a paper on top, do you think it would have

burned?
— Of course!
— But we didn't get burned.
— And why?
— We were getting ready for it all day long. We spent the whole day changing the belief that the hot coal burns our skin by the belief that we could walk on it harmlessly. And it worked. What's more, how many of us were there?
— I heard around 8,000.
— 8,000 people thought a different thought to what they had before and we were all able to do something the rest of the world believes impossible because it's scientifically proven that hot coal burns your skin if you touch it.
— Can we move that hill over there and bring it home?
— Do you think you can?
— No! That's impossible!
— That's why you won't be able to do it. But I've read and heard about other impossible things to happen, such as one person being seen in two places at the same time.
— Where they twins?
— No. the same person. It's called bilocation.
— That's cool, mate! I could be at school and playing at home.
— If they could, I think we all could, but we don't believe in that possibility with absolute certainty and that makes it impossible.
— Perhaps they were magicians.

— Perhaps. Magicians make us see things that seem impossible.
— But they are tricks. I watched a video in YouTube where they explained how they did a trick.
— The other day, I watched one of Dynamo's videos. He did some trick with the cards and as he finished, he hid behind a curtain and… disappeared!
— I'm sure there was a hole in the floor.
— I don't think so, because he performed this at a friends' place, not on stage. My guess is that when Dynamo thought "I want to walk behind a curtain and disappear. What I have in front of me is glass floor to ceiling, in an apartment where I can't go to before I prepare my trick, my body does not go through solid objects and I can't turn myself into a fly".
— A fly! Awesome!
— However, he was certain of what he wanted to get. Like me with my Audi. I wished for my Audi, didn't have the money for it nor a stable job that would allow me to save for it. But instead of telling myself 'this is impossible' and remove the photo from the fridge, I chose to tell myself 'I'm so looking forward to the things that will unfold in front of me so I can finally see this car at my doorstep'.
— Could you not ask the bank for the money?
— But you need to give it back to them.
— Ahh.
— So, my hallucination is that Dynamo knew where he wanted to get and then he'd get ideas to try. Some would get them closer to the

outcome and some not so close. Do you know what a Muse is?
— To be funny.
— Apart from that, Muses are mythological beings that inspire people; they blow ideas inside their heads. When an artist creates a fantastic work, we say he or she were very inspired or that the Muses were with them.
— And they tell them the answers in exams?
— Sure they do. It's a matter of letting your head a bit aside and let yourself go, trust, move to your heart, focus, listen and write.
— What a mess!
— Do you remember that time we were going to granny's, you asked me to take a shortcut? I told you it was better to take that alley and then we met with a friend of mine I hadn't seen for ages. She was that lady with a little dog in a bag.
— Yes! I remember! A very chubby dog that looked like Sausage[3]!
— The very same. You see? With my head, I knew that was not the shortest way, but I felt I had to take that alley. That's intuition. Things go smoothly when I follow my intuition.
— So they talk in your head?
— Sometimes, I have thoughts that go against logical or rational thinking. I think those come from the heart.
— Like what?
— Look: one day, I was at the airport and I was just about to go through the arch, one of those where it seems you need to pass

---

[3] Sausage is our cat. It's white. The dog was white too.

through nearly naked, and you need to show your toiletries and computers and they take bottles away from you.

— Do you remember that boy who had a toy gun and his mother didn't know and they stopped everything and the police was just about to get them arrested?

— What a scare! She didn't know what to do. I think she saw herself in jail! Yes, that's what I mean. So I walked into the area and there were two queues. I felt I had to go to the one on the right hand side but I counted the number of people and there were less in the one on the left, so I went to this one. Guess what happened.

— What?

— What?

— Hold on! This is the best part! *Die, motherf\*cker, die... bye/bye, motherf\*cker, bye, ahh/Go to sleep, bitch (what!)...*

— Thank you!

— In the queue I chose, the one on the left, four passengers in wheelchairs appeared out of nowhere and they went through the control before me. You can't imagine how long it took to get them through!

— Did you go to the other queue?

— No, because it was a lot longer then.

— What a fail.

— Indeed. It was a great lesson, though. Ever since, any time I feel it's better to go against what common sense says, or rational mind, I don't doubt and follow my intuition. It's never failed me.

— Well, I feel we could go on an excursion rather than to school, which is the common thing to do.
— Nice try! Sure you're right, son, and we could learn a lot more in a forest than in school today. But we can go on Saturday. What about that? We can get up a bit early and we can go to that beautiful forest where we saw a deer.
— Get up... early? On Saturday? What if we go closer by?
— We don't need to decide right now. We'll talk about it on Friday.
— Here we are. Kiss. Muah! Muuuah! Have a great day, kids.
— You too.
— You too.
— I love you.
— Love you.

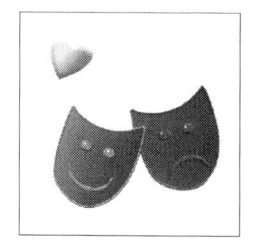

## 3. STORIES

## Context

What story do you tell yourself? Mine is "I'm not enough". No matter what I do, I always have the feeling that any accomplishment is just minor, that anyone could have done what I did so I'm not special at all, that I should have done better, that the outcome is not perfect... you get the picture.

Words are extremely powerful and they become reality. 'The word became flesh' is exactly that, the materialisation of the word, of thought. Therefore, my story is not 'I'm not enough' anymore; it used to be, but I have decided to turn it into 'fantastic things happen to me every day', I deserve all the good in my life' and the like. I must confess I've got to go little by little, because if I dare to say 'I'm wonderful', I get a bit of a short circuit in my brain. But I'll get there.

I like listening and make connections between what I hear people say and the results I see in their lives. They say success leaves clues. Success understood as happiness, as fulfilment, as inner peace. Who's in for a successful life?

At this very moment, I'm on board of an airplane; the 7$^{th}$ one I'm taking in the last 12 days.

My kids are awaiting me at the airport. I can choose to summarise my trip the way white sheep do –the masses, the bulk of society– or the way black sheep do, i.e., those who choose the bright side, the growth; to embrace the change and leave mediocrity behind.

I'll have a black sheep conversation with them and will transcribe it after it happens, and, as a case study, I'll also write the fictional white sheep conversation.

Please, walk in your children's shoes and imagine what their foundations of life would be for them if they choose to focus on the bright side of things or they choose to focus on the negative side of it all. If they are fed with positivity daily, what kind of adults will they be like? What will they teach their children? What example will they be giving to the world?

Who would you prefer to be around with? The black sheep or the white sheep? Clue: mass media feed white sheep with horror stories and bad news... all the freaking time!

## Chatting with Jamie and Mario on the way back from the airport

The black sheep story

— *Guys! I'm so happy to see you!*

— Mum!

— Mamasita!

— I was so looking forward to seeing you! I missed you terribly. I thought of you every single day and I thought 'Gosh! There are so many places I'm travelling too. I'd love to bring the children here with me'. And I also thought about the trips we've made together and how we can make many more. If you like.

— I've taken pictures and videos of places and things I thought you'd like to see. I can show you when we get home, if that's ok.

— Super cool!

— Did you have a good time while I was away?

— We got our hair cut and we went to granny's in the weekend.

— And we went mountain hiking one day too.

— I love that you have some men's time and you enjoy dad's company. If you like, on Saturday, we could go to that vegetarian restaurant you like so much.

— Oh, can we?

— Cool!

— How was your trip?

— Very exciting. See? Within 12 days, I've been in London, Estonia, London again, Las Vegas, London for the 3rd time and now, here. 7 different time zones and three different currencies in such a short time. A record for me!

— Are you tired?

— Well, I'm a big jet lagged, but since I have no boss, tomorrow I can sleep as much as I need to catch up and organise my day as I please. There's nothing as urgent as not to wait for a day or so.

– So, can we watch a movie together tonight?

– With popcorn?

– Would it be ok if we watch it tomorrow? Tonight, I have a Skype call with a French guy who's looking forward to open our business in France and then, another one with my beloved Polish team. I'm looking forward to you meeting these guys; wait and see how beautiful they are and how big their hearts are.

– Sure. Tomorrow then.

– Can we watch Terminator's last movie?

– Great idea. We missed it in the cinema. I can't wait to watch it with you.

– What else did you do?

– I got to meet a group of wonderful people and I held with them very deep and meaningful conversations. They really touched my heart. I've very good friends, even though I didn't get to spend that much time with them. I've created very strong relationships.

– Is that good for the business?

– Businesses are based on relationships between people. My purpose is, whatever the business I'm in, to establish relationships where everyone wins. My business consists on get everybody to benefit and everyone's life to improve. No less!

– So did you make friends? Do you have photos?

– In Estonia, I met a group of handsome, tall, intelligent, healthy, blond and huge hearted young fellows who not only wish to change the world and make a difference, they are completely committed to it and they are already working for it. I asked them whether they were thinking on organising summer camps for children, because I'd love you two to spend time with them.

— What do they speak?

— Estonian. But also English, so no problem.

— Let's go, then.

— Done deal! We can start making plans for the summer then.

— Yippee!

— What about Las Vegas? Is it cool?

— Yes! It's pretty much like in the movies, but with more casinos that you can imagine. From the air, you can see the town limits and then, the desert. Pure sand desert. Casinos have hotels, or the other way around, and many also have shopping centres. They are open 24/7.

— So they gamble all the time?
— Once, I woke up in the middle of the night and went downstairs just to see what the casino was like at 3 am. And yes, there were a lot of people around the tables and the slot machines. And they let them smoke there.
— Yuk! Disgusting!
— And what else do they do there?
— There are many shows, even in the streets. It's very entertaining to see the fountains and the volcano and the way many people are dressed and the limousines and so many lights all over the place. You see, I won't probably choose Las Vegas as my first destination for a holiday, but I must say it's a very entertaining place and, definitely, an option to spend a few days in a complete different fashion.
— Did you do anything fun?
— One night, after the event, we were invited to a suit in the hotel.

It was massive, guys! So big! There were more than a hundred of us and there was still so much space!

— Awesome!

— It had a round bed that turned around, most of the walls were glass walls so you can the whole town moving in front of your very eyes.

— How cool.

— Do you have pictures?

— I do indeed. I even recorded a video so you could see the place. There was also a swimming pool, on the 14th floor!

— What?

— Will you take us there?

— Sure! Sometime. It must be a top notch place, because Beyoncé was there, giving a concert.

— Did you attend it?

— It was a private one they organised in one of the big swimming pools. I could hear it from my room, though.

— Did you give a seminar in Las Vegas?

— No, I didn't. I attended a conference organised by a sister company. The speakers are very open and kind. A great example to learn from them, not only how to talk from stage but how to teach a lot of content, with high value and a sense of humour, also being able to reach all different levels in the crowd. A huge pleasure.

— Did you do a lot of business?

— As I told you before, I made very good relationships and strengthened others and that's the foundation of life and business. And made new friends, which is cool. I'm sure some businesses will come out of this, but even if it didn't, I've learned a lot and gained a lot.
— Where else did you go to? I can't remember all the places you said before.

— London. 3 full days in between the trips. I spent each night in a different place, so I could see different parts of the city. I love London; it's so lively and there are so many people from so many places, so many colours...
— Do they paint their faces? They didn't when I went there.
— I didn't see anyone with their faces painted either.
— Sorry. I meant they are from many backgrounds, races, ways

of living, cultures, costumes... See what I mean?

— Ok. I see now.

— We have a surprise for you at home.

— Great! I've brought you some bottle caps for you collection. I think you don't have them. I've been thinking that we could also prepare a special mango and banana smoothie. What do you think?

— Or we could go to for a paella on Sunday, yes?

— Even better. Both. Can I give you another hug?

— No! two!

— With a kiss!

The white sheep story

— Guys! I'm so happy to see you!
— Mum!
— Mamasita!
— I was so looking forward to seeing you! I missed you a lot. Every night, before I went to sleep, I thought about you and felt terribly guilty for not being with you. And I kept wondering what I was doing there. Was I doing it for the money? Did it make sense? Wouldn't I be much better off if I were home with my kids, the most important thing in my life?
— ...
— I took some pictures and videos of things that you'd have liked to see, because, right now, I can't afford taking you with me so you can see them by yourselves.
— But we're fine...
— I know dad looks after you very well and I know you don't need me at all, so if I die, you'd be fine, you'd continue with your life.
— But you're not dying, right?
— Well, you never know!
— ...
— How was your trip?
— Exhausting! In 12 days, I've been in 7 different time zones, 3

different currencies, carrying work clothes and casual clothes for summer and winter weather plus for air conditioned, which is a different animal altogether. I didn't enjoy a single free day at all and now, here I am, all jet lagged on a Tuesday, so I still have to work for three full days before the weekend, with a lot of work to catch up plus new work from the trip.

— Can we watch a movie together tonight?

— With popcorn?

— I wish! I have two meetings, I mean, two webinars. With a French guy I met only last summer but I can't even remember what he looks like and then with the Polish guys.

— Sorry.

— What else did you do?

— The truth of the matter is that I didn't do that much. I feel terrible because I have the impression I wasted a lot of time and invested a lot of the company's money for very little results.

— So you didn't make any new client?

— Well, yes, we did. In Estonia, we've created an investment club with some young fellows. I think they know more than I do and they all were taller, healthier, blonder and more intelligent than me. Not a great place for low self-esteem, not at all.

— What do they speak?

— Estonian, but every single one of them spoke English as well, so there was no need to translate anything. And there I was, feeling I was not needed and feeling my presence was not necessary at all.

— But you're very good at what you do.
— I think I've lost my touch. It didn't last long!
— What about Las Vegas? Is it cool?
— The flight was 11 hours in a row. Very tiresome. The temperature there was boiling hot outdoors and freezing cold indoors because they set the air conditioned at very low temperatures, lower than we'd here set the heating at. I can't understand it!
— Did you visit any casino?
— Yes. I visited a few of them, because Las Vegas is just lots of casinos and hotels and all hotels have a casino.
— And can you walk into the casinos just like that?
— Well, the entrance to the hotels is through the casinos. And they make it all very easy for people to gamble and spend money. Everything is designed for people to spend and waste their money; they get their brains washed and they fill up their lives with things that have no value. It's like zombie land.
— Like *The Walking Dead*?
— Yeah... Pretty much.
— Did you do anything fun?
— One night, after the event, we were invited to spend some time networking. What I wanted the most was going to my room and have a rest, but there was no option. The gathering was in a massive suite, so big it even had a swimming pool. On a 14th floor!
— Wow! Cool!
— But what's the point, when the hotel has several swimming pools

available? Plus renting that sort of villa inside a hotel costs thousands per night. What a huge waste!
— Do you have pictures?
— I took them so you'd focus on what's important in life and what's obscene.
— Will you take us there?
— Never! Las Vegas is all false and wasting money. Imagine that a group of people hired Beyoncé for a private concert at this hotel. A private concert! I can't imagine how expensive that was! And for what? To show off they attended a private concert with a rock star? So vane! Plus the volume was so high, of course it was, it was impossible to go to sleep until it ended, around 3 am.
— So you heard the concert?
— Damn I did! No other option!
— Ok...
— Did you give a seminar in Las Vegas?
— No. I attended a conference organised by a sister company of ours. They are very nice, but I didn't have that much time to talk to them and I couldn't understand their talks very well, because I don't know enough of what they teach to follow it all. Besides, I'm not used to their accents, so I kept missing a lot of information and felt terrible about it; I felt stupid.
— Did you do a lot of business?
— Our partners in the US will be handling most of it. I still can't see what I went there for. They could have handled it all by themselves and I could have given them a hand from here. What a

lot of time and money we could have saved! And I could have been with you two during the weekend... and having a rest, which I need so much!

— Where else did you go to? I can't remember all the places you said before.

— I was in London. 3 days but not in a row. I was dragging the suitcase up and down all the time. And the visits to London were not so worth it, because many of the meetings were cancelled. We were cancelled the biggest one of them that, potentially, could have brought more clients to the upcoming Wales event. A bit of a fail, as you say.

— We have a surprise for you at home.

— I feel so bad! I didn't bring you anything! I didn't have any spare time. I feel awful, boys. I even considered bringing you some chocolate, because that's easy to buy at the airports and I wouldn't be here empty handed, but I know you prefer to eat more healthily. As for myself, I've eaten more than I should have, because I was attending so many meetings, and I now feel fat and a glutton.

— You look just like when you left.
— As fat and old?
— Same pretty.
— Can I have a hug?
— And me too?
— Of course, children.

# 4. WAS I EVER A CHILD?

## Context

Right after turning 13, Mario asked me this question: would I prefer to live 70 years as an adult, never knowing what being a child was like or 70 years as a child, never knowing what being an adult was like.

What a question!

One of the stories I tell myself is that my childhood was unhappy. My only one sister got married and left home to live very far away (4 hours away by train, huge distance from my perspective of 4 feet tall back in the early 70's) and I was left alone with a mother who considered herself an old woman at 38 and with a father 10 years older than her. Applying her definition, he was ancient; I was 6.

My father spent months in a row without talking and he was violent. And alcoholic. My mother's profile, I learned a lot later, matched perfectly with my father's; it's called co-dependence.

I felt trapped in the middle of a battlefield in a war that was not mine but that I undoubtedly chose. That's the way I learned how not to be a parent!

I also know now that the moment I leave all that old story behind, I will be a lot happier. I am certain I'll get there and that very day, I'll be completely FREE.

I give my children all I didn't get from my parents that I missed so much.

They say we give and teach what we want to get and learn; that keeps the energy moving around.

## A few words with Mario on our way to granny's

— Mum, if you could choose between living 70 years as an adult and never have been a girl or living 70 years as a girl and never be an adult, what would you pick?
— Well... I'm guessing it depends on the circumstances.
— As a girl or as an adult.
— If it were like a girl with the kind of life you're having now, as a girl, no doubt! But I do prefer my life as an adult now to the life I had as a child.
—...?
— I think you're a very happy boy, son.

— I am!

— You can be a child.

— That's because I am a child.

— With us, at home, you're free to do whatever you want. You can play, eat anything we have at home, watch a movie if you feel like it, use the telephone, switch on the lights, take a shower, tell jokes, lie down in the sofa, turn the heating on, bring friends over... And you know that whatever you say or do, we'll never get mad at you.

— Of course, mum!

— It was not like that in my home.

— Was it not?

— My dad would spend months in a row not talking to my mother or to me and when he eventually decided to talk to us, any topic could make him go extremely angry, and violent quite often, and he would turn mute again for some other months.

— Oh.

— In the silence periods, he could start a fight any time, scream and behave violently. For any reason; for any unreasonable tiny little thing. I grew up in a state of constant fear.

— ...

— I know you find it hard to imagine something like this.

— Yeah.

— Is it ok if I give you more information about all this? I don't want to burden you.

— Sure. Keep going.
— My father never gave the first step to give me a kiss. He let himself being kissed and, quite often, he pretended he was asleep when I kissed him goodnight and he was watching telly. And he never ever gave me a hug.
— Never?
— Never. In 29 years.
— ...
— Once, as a baby, he fed me pure. I couldn't walk yet but I still remember it. And my mother confirmed it. That was the only one time he fed me. He never gave me a bath, put me to bed, brought me to school, attended a school play, he never met my teachers. Nothing.
— Oh.
— Will I tell you more? Are you ok?
— I'm fine!
— Sure?
— Sure! Bring it on, babe!
— Some Sunday mornings, he would leave home and wouldn't tell where he was heading to. Sometimes, my mother would tell me to go with him. We would take a bus in one end of the town we lived in and would go to the other end, to one of those sort of pubs where you can be outside as well. The ride would take around 40 minutes and he never said a word in any of the rides.
— Nothing? You were both quiet all the time?

— All the time. When we go there, he would order a glass of wine. Or more. He would never asked me what I wanted, so I never had anything or tap water, if I asked for it. If there were see-saws, that was great, because it was always very early in the morning, there was nobody else there, no kids, so I had the swings all for myself. Luxurious!

— Didn't you have swings when you were little?

— Only in one park and my mum used to say that was a waste of time, so she hardly ever took me there.

— And... what did you do if there were no see-saws?

— With my dad, you mean?

— Yeah.

— If I had time enough to get a book before he closed the door without me, I would have the company and entertainment of a book.

— I see.

— Then, some other 40 minutes of silence and, when at home, my mother would question me for a long while: where had we been, with whom, what did he have...

— ...

— I felt like a spy. I felt used.

— What else did you do?

— Every now and then, we would only travel downtown. He used to take me to an arts exhibition and afterwards, he would treat me to a Spanish tortilla tapa. They tasted so good!

— Better than the ones at *The Tizón*?

— No way! Theirs, apart from being exquisite, I have them with the two of you. No comparison whatsoever!

— They're the best ones!

— Indeed they are.

— Now that I think of it, whenever we saw art, paintings, sculptures, he would then say something about it. He was an artist himself. He was very good at drawing, engraving, at perspective and theory of art. He was also a wood artist and made beautiful pieces of furniture.

— Did he paint pictures too?

— I remember seeing drawings, with colour pencils. They look fantastic to my eyes. But I think now that his self-esteem was so low he would never consider arts as a serious career. He was a civil servant and always worked for a salary.

— Do you have any of his drawings?

— I remember a drawing he did copying a portrait of mine on my first communion day. But I grew to disliking him so much that I chose not to have anything from him.

— I see.

— He died 20 years ago. Not that long ago, I finally understood he did what he could. And he taught me a very powerful lesson: how to treat my children: by doing exactly the opposite he did!

— I love you a lot, mum.

— I know, sweet heart. And I feel so so grateful because you chose me as your mum. And I love chatting with you and to see

that you're so happy in this home of ours, and I love it when you laugh and I see you feel so free and joyful.
— Yes.
— When I visited my grandparents as a child, with my aunt and uncle and my cousins all living together, I used to be very happy there too. There were no fights, we all ate at the same time, we could come and go, we shared it all. That's the house in the country we go every now and then, where my god mother lives and my cousin has so many cows.
— Yeah, I know.
— I think we built this house of ours in the country because my best memories as a child belong to the time I spent at my grandparents'.
— And because we can make noise here and have cats.
— Besides. Anyway, I want to make very clear to you that my childhood was nothing compared with most children's in the world. Millions of them don't even have food, or live in war; others are bullied and, yet worse again, abused… by their own relatives. We're so lucky to live as rich people.
— Are we rich?
— I believe it's half the people in the planet live with less than 1$ a day.
— One dollar? Is that all?
— And half of the population lives with less than 100$ per month. Only slightly above what we pay every time we refill the tank.
— Wow!

– One out of three has no access to a sewage system.
– What is it? A loo?
– Loo, shower, running water. Look at all the taps we have at home.
– Yesterday, Leo was drinking from one of them because it was dripping.
– Look at that. Here, even cats are rich.
– Cool.
– But you know what might happen?
– What?
– That some years from now, you'll be telling your girlfriend or boyfriend, or your own children, that when you were a child, your mum used to say or do this or that and that's something that hurt you deeply and... you need some therapy of some sort to sort it all out.
– I don't know...
– No, not necessarily. You're learning now to be aware of the stories that we tell ourselves. You see? I can choose to dwell on my childhood to be a very unhappy one or I can choose to feel grateful for the lessons that I learned and how I'm enjoying my children now. I can choose to be the in the present and only use the past to learn and then let it go. Does it make sense?
– I guess...
– Too complicated?
– What?
– Exactly. What. Nothing is complicated unless we choose to see it

that way. I love you, son, and I learn so much from you!
— Although you know so many things?
— I do know many things. I studied and learned a lot, but you figure it all out by yourself. You make it simple. The trick is what you do all the time naturally.
— What do I do?
— Be here. Now. In the moment.
— Like the fish in *Nemo*, the one that didn't remember anything?
— In a way... you see, I think unhappiness comes from worrying about what hasn't happened yet and from trying to change the past.
— ...
— I know. It doesn't make sense.
— Do we go?
— Sure! I'll take a shower and we can go. Give me a hug, will you?
— ...
— Um! You smell so good!
— You too, mum.
— Love you, son.
— Me too. Legit.

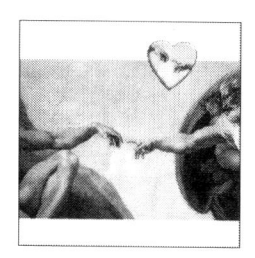

## 5. GOD! I CAN'T BELIEVE THIS!

### Context

I grew up in a traditionally catholic country. The way I perceive society was around me was pretty much hypocritical: playing the movie that everything and everyone in the family was perfect out there and hiding all the crap behind a closed door.

On top of that, my mother's top values were the observation of certain commandments of the bible and make sure anything I did was righteous so I wouldn't be the topic of any conversation outside our home.

Only now, while writing this text, have I discovered our commandments in Latino countries are different to those in the Anglo-speaking word. We, Latinos, have manage blend together the commandments about god, have no other gods before him and have no idols, in just one so we would have a spare one to use... where? In sex! This way, the simple commandment of *you shall not commit adultery* splits into two: 1) you shall not commit unchaste actions and 2) you will not allow unholy thoughts and actions.

Number 5 (4 for us): *You will honour your father and your mother.* In the context I grew up in, as a baby boomer, these words were the cover hiding the obligation of putting up with anything parents threw on their children, of not answering back ever, of allowing abuse in any shape or form, of always agreeing with them and never say no, of being always last, of not being listened to, of obeying blindly, of asking for permission for anything. Once the children moved out, this commandment translated into calling the parents daily on the phone, having Sunday dinners with them, letting them decide on what's best for our children, taking important decisions with top priority of not displeasing them, and, eventually, taking care of them when old and sick, always with a bright smile and lots of love, even though the price for that is our own health and life.

Then, two commandments to keep us away from sex in any shape of form: thoughts, desire, actions. In short: deny our nature.

Since Mother Nature has her own rules, staying away from what's in our core, those obeying the human rules would end up frustrated and even impotent or frigid. Those not following the human rules would feel dirty, guilty... and those who conceived a child under the embarrassment of a proof of how they've sinned would be marked forever, so would the baby, what a start!

Again, this was when I grew up and as a generalisation. Luckily enough, the black sheep of every family were clever enough to follow their hearts. Many of these black sheep were admired and envied later in life; others were hated. Over all, by the sisters that stayed at home taking care of their parents, with no free time whatsoever, poor quality of life and, as a result, not the best mood and health.

It took me two years to completely disengage from the Catholic church. Two solid years until I stopped hearing all the bells in the world calling to mass on Sundays. Two full years feeling guilty for not complying with every single rule of this rite and it took me even a bit longer than that to remove from my cells the fear of eternal condemnation. The secret? Changing the information I had loaded as my programming with other information that makes me happier, more fulfilled, from where I can enjoy life because is in alignment with my true self.

I bring up my children in the spirituality, but outside any religion. It's up to them to decide if they wish to join any church or not.

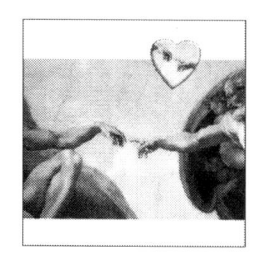

## Going for a walk with Jamie by the beach on a Sunday morning

— Do we walk over there, as it's sunnier?

— Sure, mom.

— Listen. Those are the bells of that church over there. Do we go to mass?

— That's... that's a joke, right?

— Did you know that I used to be a catholic and attended mass every Sunday?

— Oh. Did you? I didn't know. And, what did you go for?

— Because going to mass every Sunday and every catholic festivity was one of the 15 rules we had to follow.

— What rules?

— They were organised in two groups and they were called 'commandments'. 10 of them are the general ones and then there's another group of 5 which relate to church.

— Well. It doesn't seem too many things to remember.

— It was a bit tricky, you know? There was a lot of stuff hidden behind the 10 commandments.

— Like what?

— My school was an ultra-Catholic one. They had this little book that was a sort of collection of nearly all the sins that could be confessed. When us girls went to confession, we were given some time to search for possible deviations to the rules in our behaviour, that is, sins. Remember that we talked about sin the other day in the car?

— Yeah. It was when you did something that others said it was wrong and you had to feel guilty for it.

— More or less. Although what I think now is that this right and wrong thing is only humans make up. What if things just are?

— But if you kill somebody, you go to jail.

— That would be against one of the commandments, which is *you shall not kill* and that would be considered a mortal sin.

— Sure. Because the other fellow dies.

— I believe they are called mortal because if you commit one of this mortal sins and you die before confessing and regretting it, you'd go straight to hell.

— And they burn you up?

— In movies, hell normally looks like a place full of demons, with fire all over the place and they burn those who did bad things. But, you know? I don't really get why demons would first tempt people to do bad things and then burn them in hell for doing the very thing that brought you there in the first place?

— Sounds silly alright. Maybe they bet?

— Excellent idea! Perhaps there's a competition between angels and demons, to see who gets more souls. Listen: angels offer heavens after dead and hardships during this life on earth; demons offer treats in this life, like money and luxurious things and women and good luck and, in exchange, people gave up their souls and, when they die, the demons burn their souls.

— I don't know what I'd go with... I can't understand why we can't have it all!

— Because in this religion that once was my own, as I understood it, anyway, they convinced us that we always had to choose between one thing or another. That's because Catholicism is based on scarcity, again, as I understood it. They brain washed us so we would associate abundance with guilt.

— I see.

— Do you know when the penny dropped and I finally realised I always thought this or that, rather than this <u>and</u> that?

— When we kept two kittens instead of just one?

— Very close. It was one day when I asked your brother, when he was very little, he would be 3 or 4 then I'm guessing, so when I asked him what cat he like better, Mixta or Egg. And he said he liked both.

— I like both too.

— I know! That's so obvious to me now! But I grew up in the (false) belief that I always had to choose and have an opinion about every single thing and everything figured out as good or bad. Hold on. It gets even funnier! The hypothetical questions we were asked to set this wiring system of good and bad were normally negative, like *what do you prefer, being deaf or being blind?*

For instance, when I went on holidays when I was in my 30's, my mother would ask me always the same question: 'Are you ok? No accidents? As long as nothing bad happens, everything else is meaningless'. I agree to a certain point, but any joy is wiped off the table. I would have loved to be asked something more in the lines of 'did you have a good time?', 'what did you learn?', 'have you met interesting people?'

— She always asks us if we've had a good time.
— Good news! She's learned!

For me, religion was something a bit like that: the good is the absence of bad and no joy whatsoever.

— What's that of confession?

— During any class, a girl would knock on the door to announce Father So-and-So was available for confessions. So we were allowed to go to the school's chapel, read the little book and tell the priest all the things that we had done wrong, according to that book.

— And you could play hooky?

— Part of it. Maybe some girls didn't end up in the chapel, I don't know. But going back to that book: there was a chapter per commandment with lots of questions addressing different shapes of sins against each commandment. For instance, under the *you shall not kill*, you could find this question among many others: 'have you smoked?'

— Smoking is a sin??

— It goes against life so, for them, it is. Also calling people names was listed under this chapter, as insults go against the integrity of another person.

— So you were burned in hell if you called prick to your brother, even though he was a prick and deserves it?

— That would be considered as a venial sin, a minor sin. With those, you don't go to hell, but when you die, they used to send you to a place called 'purgatory', which was something like a prison where you did time for your crimes. The more minor sins, the more time in purgatory. Now, a pope has declared that purgatory is obsolete, so there's no purgatory anymore.

— Does that make sense?

— I can't explain it with my rational mind. Not only that, but a lot of it. But, you see, back then, it was all I knew and I bought it all.

— Ok. So what happened when you told the priest all those things?

— If you really and deeply regretted what you had done wrong, the priest would say a prayer I never understood because he spoke very fast, he would tell you what prayers to say as a sort of punishment and if you complied with the whole lot, you could walk out of there with a clean soul.

— So... could you do anything bad as long as you told the priest afterwards?

— You know? I always have that impression: that Catholics could do anything, absolutely anything, and as far as they told a priest and they felt remorse and regret, they could always start from scratch again.

— So you wouldn't go to jail?

— If they catch him or her, of course they would go to jail. But anything said to a priest in confession cannot be used in court, because it's a secret.

— Yes! I remember now! I saw it in a movie! This man walked into a church and told a priest in a box that he had killed another man and they brought that priest to court and he didn't tell anything and the jury said the man was not guilty because there was not enough evidence. I thought that was outrageous, because I didn't know this thing of not being allowed to tell a jury the truth. And what else was a sin?

— I hardly remember any of the questions, and there were more than 100. But I do remember other things we used to do: at the beginning of each period, we said a prayer. The prayer at noon was a bit longer and every day in the month of May, we prayed a rosary every day.

— What's that?

— In summary, you say a title and then a prayer —our father, who's art in heaven...—, then 10 Hail Mary's, which is another prayer and finally, another one. At the end of 5 of these cycles, something called a litany.

— Everything was repeated so many times?

— Yes. Over and over.

— And how does it work?

— They used to tell us to set an intention before we started. For instance, hunger.

— So there would be more hunger? That's weird.

— You're such a smart ass! Can you believe I only realised that only a few years ago? Where attention goes, energy flows and results show, so if we were praying for 'hunger', I'm guessing we were producing more of it.

— Sure. But that's what you tell us all the time.

— I know, sweet. You see? This is relatively new for me. Just as well I learned it in time to teach you!

— Yeah.

— I know how silly it may sound to you, but there was no internet in my times. I watched a video by Gregg Braden, where he talks about the different kinds of prayers. One of them is repeating prayers. In my experience, since we said those prayers so many times, we knew them upside down and we could be telling them without thinking, so our thoughts would normally wander around.
— And what other ways?
— Another way was to tell god that if he fulfilled what we were asking for, then we'd something for him, such as some pilgrimage, or attend extra masses, or give away some money to those in need or things like that.
— Like a deal?
— A bit like a deal, yes.
— There were other forms of praying but the one that made more sense to me, and I've found in many other places also, was imagining that what we pray for, we already have it. Then, you see it all with your mind's eye, with a lot of detail, feeling it, hearing it, smelling it, living the experience. Having the certainty that it's already there but also letting it go, as if it doesn't happen, that's cool because something better is on the way for me.
— I thought it was always like this.
— Is that how you do it, son, how you pray?
— I... don't... really pray. I just think things.
— Can you elaborate a bit on this, please? Like, how do you start your day.
— First thing, I take a shower.

— I know! I mean, do you plan your day ahead, your week ahead, your year, your life?
— More like the day. While I'm in the shower and the water runs over my body, I look at the thoughts that cross my mind, whichever ones they are. They could be something that happened yesterday, or before, or will happen and I just see them.
— Do you look at them very closely?
— No. I just see them. I look at them and they pass by.
— They don't upset you?
— Nope.
— Does anything upset you, sweet?
— Not really. Maybe at the time something is happening, but that's it. After that, I just see what happened and they go.
— You only observe them, right?
— Yeah.
— Jamie! I've been working hard to get to be the observer of my existence for more than half my life, and you're there at 15!
— Really?
— Really, yes. I'm so delighted for you. More questions, I'm curious. What do you think god is like? What could you call the higher force in the spiritual realm?
— I think it's an *it*, not a he or a she. And I think it's, like, split in different parts, parts of the same thing but separated at the same time. I don't really know how to explain it.
— Like subcontractors of some sort?

— Like a starfish: you can cut the individual arms and each one will grow a new individual but each arm is part of the first individual. I don't know how to put it in words.

— And what's each one of the arms?

— Each arm is in charge of a different thing and controls it.

— Like one arm is in charge of the galaxies and another one of the arthropods?

— No: one is in charge of happiness and another one of anger and so on.

— So by 'things' you mean 'emotions', right?

— That's it. Emotions. It's hard for me to explain. I can see it in my head, but I don't know how to communicate it.

— You're doing great, it's just that I want to confirm I'm understanding what you say correctly.

— Ok.

— So, if I understand well, you're saying to me a higher power is in charge of our emotions. So, we're completely at their mercy?

— No. It creates the emotions and everything else and people have the will to choose one or another. It only displays them and makes them happen so they're available for us and it's up to us what to do with it all.

— Wow. Very deep. Thank you. So, when you wish for something, how do handle this?

— Like what?

— Let's say you wish to get to know Eminem personally. He lives nearly 4,000 miles apart from you and doesn't even know you exist. Where would you start?

— I would think that I want to get to know him and then I just listen to whatever thoughts come to my mind and act on them.
— Would it be accurate you listen to your heart and find the way and the answers there.
— Yeah. It would. Anything I need, I listen inside myself.
— And everything it's there.
— Basically, yes. But then I do what I need to, like look something up in Google or go somewhere or something and then I find the next clue.
— So you're telling me for you to get your goals, you follow the indications you get inside and follow the clues as if they were part of a gymkhana.

— You're making me laugh now! I never saw it this way but, yes, that would be very accurate to say.

— I take my hat off, son! I'm in awe of you! All the seminars and therapies I've attended, and I read so many books, and you come to me with a comprehensive live application of it all!

— Are you comparing me with an a pp?

— They wish!

— Oh! Thank you!

— Hold on. It was the previous street. We need to walk back now. Let's cross the road.

— Thanks! I'm going to order a mango juice.

— I will order nachos.

— I love you, son.

— I love you too, mum.

# 6. WHAT WILL I BE WHEN I GROW UP? or ¿QUÉ SERÁ, SERÁ?

## Context

This was a very frequent question when I was a child. Not only that, our parents were asked the question as if we, children, were not right there, in front of the enquirer.

With the perspective of time, I think now that it was a question born to satisfy the need for labelling every member of the flock from the very time that we were just little chicks in the nest. Adults felt a lot safer if they could catalogue every creature, from an early age, and classify in the right box, shelf and wardrobe.

Not only that, if the answer they got from somebody else's child corresponded to a lower shelf than their Richie's, yet better again. So if Richie's parents asked Peter what he was going to be when he grew up and Peter, obediently, would answer he'd be a lawyer, Richie's parents would smile understandingly because Richie was going to be a judge. Poor Peter, he'd be living his life from a lower shelf. Extra brownie points would be on the table if Richie's parents could add 'like his dad and his grandad' after the 'judge' bit.

In many stiff families, this celebration of their Richie's future accomplishments would not come to fruition. Let's take a look at some possible scenarios:

  a) Richie spent his youth studying something he hated, he feels trapped, his relationship with his parents is only a masquerade and he can't understand why he's not feeling happy when he's achieved all life is about (allegedly).
  b) Richie can't stand the pressure and seeks the help of some kind of drug to be able to put with it all.
  c) Richie, on a sunny morning, decides to take control of his life, moves into his hidden boyfriend's apartment and changes the robe and the gavel by a guitar and a microphone, his true passion.

Back then —I'm a baby boomer— the theory was that parents wanted their children to be 'more'. Achieve more than they had achieved, more than their parents had achieved, more than other children would achieve. All this would be measured by the Money scale, quite precise, and two others a bit more subjective: Prestige and Social Class. In general, the Happiness scale was nowhere to be seen.

That was the theory. A closer look to this master plan shows many a tense relationship between parents and children, were due to parents giving it all away for their children, which ended up with jealousy, resentment, lack of appraisal, anger, all of the above. And these parents aren't even conscious of it.

If we flip the coin, we find grown children who hate what they do. They might think they chose their careers, but they just fulfilled their parent's frustrations – or not. A lot of unhappiness. Such a pity.

## A few words with Mario in bed

**Occupation: comedian**

— What's an alligator in a vest?

— I don't know...

— An in-vest-tigator!

— Wow! That's great! Did you make it up?

— Yeah. And some children from school copied me.

— Does that bother you?

— Nope. Even though they say it was their idea. But it was mine.

— Do you know what I think?

— What?

— That we only copy those we think they are better than us. So perhaps you could feel flattered.

— Oh.

— I think you're so funny, Mario...

— Na-tu-ral-ta-lent!

— Exactly! That's exactly it!

— What?

— I think you're very talented to say and do funny things. You can make jokes out of anything and everything. It comes naturally. And you do it because that's who you are; you don't tell jokes to be accepted or loved, you tell jokes and do funny things because it comes naturally to you.

—...

[4]

---

[4] This picture is not photoshopped

— Sorry, son! This might be a bit dense. But you know how I love to look into things and see what I can learn from them. I learn a lot from you.
— You do?
— Every day.
— But I'm a child and you know a lot of things!
— I do know many things, love, but you're a wise man.
— Wise men are those old people that make magic soups in a big bucket, right?
— That's the way they make them look in books and movies, yes. I think your mental image is that of a druid in a fairy tale. I have the hunch that this is something we were led to believe: that the answer to many problems could be found in a concoction in a cauldron, in a pill or in a trip to India. What I think is that a wise man asks better questions than those going to them in search of a solution.
— I understand nothing.
— When you were 6 years old, you cried every school day. This had never happened before.
— I can't remember that.
— You were sad at home and as we were getting closer to your school, you held on to us and cried and would even refuse to walk.
— And my snot ran down my nose?
— Most likely.

— Gross!
— When you came back home from school, you never told us what was going on.
— Weird!
— Eventually, we were able to break through your resistance and you confessed the reason why you didn't want to go to school was because you couldn't read or write.
— But I was only 6!
— That was the year when they taught you to read and write. However, there were two children who had learned from their parents during the summer holidays and you decided to focus your attention on those two, rather than in the remaining 21 in your class, who were illiterate, just like you.
— What a silly thing!
— I'm guessing the kind of questions you were asking yourself back then were something like 'what if I'm stupid and I never learn?', 'What if the other children in my class learn to read and write and I don't?' 'Will they stop loving me if I don't learn?' 'Will they punish me?' 'Will I have to repeat the year and they'll laugh at me?' 'Will the other children call me names?'
— Really?
— I don't know for sure, honey, but let's imagine that's what you were thinking, ok? Then, one day, you decided to visit some wise people (dad and I) and they asked you better questions. What do you think we asked you?
— No clue. Whether I was really stupid?

— Cold. We started with: don't you know that we love you the same whether you can read and write or not?

— I do, yeah.

— That's right. I mean, that was the first question. Then, we asked you: do you know this is the year when you'll learn to read and write? Do you know there are only two children that have learned so far? Do you know of any child in a higher class who hadn't learned? Things like that.

— I see.

— You had answers for all those questions. But you were all sad and cried because you were only asking yourself the questions that made you feel bad. When you started asking yourself better questions, with a little bit of help, those that filled you up with energy, you stopped crying.

— Cool.

— And you learned to read and write.

— Yeah.

— And do you know that many adults ask children what they want to be when they grow up?

— Nope.

— Well: when they ask you, if they do, know that you have no obligation whatsoever to answer.

— Ok.

— You don't even have to tell me. But, can I say something? Can I tell you what I'd like you to be?

— Sure...

— Whatever you want!

— Then... what about not going back to school?

— Well, you see, by law, you have to go for a few years. Besides, I think education gives us a wider point of view and some tools to achieve things. But there are many ways to get an education apart from school and university.

— Did you go to university?

— I did. And I had a great time. I also studied a lot, but, overall, I made very good friends and I had a fantastic time. If only because of the fun part and the friends you'll make, it might be worth it for you to go to university. You know it's entirely up to you, though, aren't you lucky?

— I suppose.

— Since you're so funny, maybe you could be a comedian. Anyone can see that the happiest people are those doing what they love doing, those devoting themselves to activities they'd do even though they weren't paid for them.

— Like what?

— Like photography, for instance. I love taking pictures and photoshop them and making books and many other things. I've taken pictures for free and also got paid for them. I will always take photographs, because I love it, I find it very fulfilling and also challenging. And I can be as creative as I want.

— Cool.

— Of course, money could be an issue.

— Remember when I was a child and I thought money came out of the ATM machines?

— I do! That was funny too. But now you're a big kid and you know there are other ways to make money.

— The stock market.

— For instance. In that seminar we attended during the summer, they told us about separating part of the money we make and invest it in what they called 'a money machine', so money works for us. Then, with the power of compound interest, we'll get to the day when we can retire and live out of the interests.

— I remember. But I don't have a job.

— But you have an allowance and tips you get from your grannies. Also, since you're young, I can teach you about some strategies to invest in the stock market so when you grow up, you can make the money in the stock market and do whatever you love doing. And, you know what?

— What?

— That as you'll be doing what you love and you'll have time and the finances you require for learning and becoming great in your area, plus you won't have the pressure of performance to make money out of it, you'll end up making even more money.

— That is cool, mama!

— Are you aware that it's uncommon that a mother encourages her son to be a comedian?

— Is it not?

— At least, it wasn't in my time.

— So... will I be able to play video games all day long?
— Would that make you happy!
— Yes!
— In the seminar this last summer, do you remember how happy those talking about their beloved projects looked? All of them had spent a lot of time, energy and money in education, plus a lot of practice. Their aim was to become the best ones in what they love doing because they felt it their call. Then, they put all of that in service of others, adding a lot of value, and everyone's happy: business people and clients. Win-win. Lots of lives changes. Freaking awesome.
— I see.
— Don't you think they wouldn't be so happy if they spent the whole day on the coach, with a remote in their hands?
— I dunno...
— Ah, c'mon!
— No, not really. But, will I be able to play when I'm a grown up?
— Of course, love! There's time for everything. It just may happen that you won't feel like playing as much as now because you could think of many other things you'd prefer to spend your time in.
— Better than playing video games?
— Things change with time, I mean, the way we see things changes with time. Do you remember when you wanted to watch *Nemo* all the time?
— Boring!

— Same with video games. Good night, my sweet. I love you.
— Me too. Good night.
— Muah!
— I love you legit, mamasita. More than any cat!
— That's so sweet, love! Thank you!

# 7. YUMMY!

## Context

Food. What a topic!

Who needs to eat? Animals, plants and other beings in other kingdoms feed themselves. They consume food, even though this food might be just air, but they do, as a way of getting energy and nutrients for being alive, growing, pass life to the next generation.

I have the notion that if we looked closely to what our brothers and sisters in nature do, our health and our shapes would change drastically.

Big question: why are there more and more fat people in the civilised world? Let me summarise a few facts I've learned lately.

Jon Gabriel talks about our FAT[5] programming. It consists on the activation of a routine to store fat, which is extremely useful for periods of less food or more cold, or while the foetus is growing inside their mothers, as is the case of mammals.

---

[5] FAT: Famine and Temperature. From his book *The Gabriel Method*.

In our so called civilised society, where we have homes, heating, supermarkets open 24/7 all year round and clothes, this FAT program happens to be redundant. However, our bodies can think there's danger out there and this thought triggers a response in the shape of... fat.

For example: if somebody in our daily life, at home or at work, is bulling us or we consider that this person is harmful for us one way or another, we grow a layer of fat to put a distance between them and us. Even if we sew up our mouths, we'll still be fat!

Please, note this is a very short summary of my interpretation of this book, which, by the way, makes a lot of sense to me.

Something else we humans do is celebrate with food. And we also eat when we're sad. And we also become allergic to certain foods; every time, there's more evidence of the relationship between these allergies and events that we lived as traumatic and took place in the past, in this life or a previous one.

More: we, humans, create tendencies and fashion in what we eat: for generations, meat was considered as the best source for protein and it was chosen as one of the best foods, chosen by athletes, sick persons, children, those working hard physically. Now, the OMS declares that the way meat is processed nowadays causes cancer. Another example: it's so good to have a cup of red wine along with lunch! Then: better not to drink while we eat. Or: we need to drink at least 2 litres of water a day versus drink only when you're thirsty.

Sometimes, the information is not complete. That's what happened with dairy products: they have calcium, which is a component of our bones, so for generations, mothers were pushing cow milk down their children's throats, whether they wanted or not. Now, it's seems that unless we do exercise and also take magnesium, the calcium in the milk doesn't get attached onto our bones; even worse: it depletes their calcium content! And... worse again! Dairy products are the worst for our nutrition!! No need to be a rocket scientist to see that no other mammal in the world drinks the milk of any other species after the unweaning. Never heard of dogs with osteoporosis.

I read somewhere, I wished I remembered where, that some monks with a lot of experience in meditation were capable of ingesting strychnine in a dose that would kill a person but had no effect whatsoever in them because they blessed what they ate.

Other things we humans do is... poison our food! In a larger or smaller extent and, of course, always fulfilling the requirements established by law.

How do we do that? We have many methods: addition of substances (chlorine to the water, fluorine to toothpaste, carcinogenic substances to creams, sprays); use of thinggie-cides (biocides, pesticides, fungicides, etc. Please, note the prefix '-cide' means 'to kill'); removing the nutrition factors from food (like we do with flour, thus baking some white stuff we call 'bread' which lacks nourishment); creating GMO's[6], who knows the effects these have and will have in the future generations; eating animals that grown under stressful conditions, fed them with substances that make them grow in record time; baking cakes with the perfect ratio of sugar and fat to nullify the chemical signal in our brains meaning 'I'm full'; selling products under the name of food and drink that are not such a thing.

I've left for last what I believe has the right to be the icing in the cake: medicines. In principle, they've been designed to heal us (as if patients had nothing to do with the healing process). The facts, however, are god-almighty-what-the-hell: check up the statistics on iatrogenic deaths lately.

I'm glad to see, though, that it is more and more frequent to find places that include smoothies in their menus and that we can actually see the fruits they prepare them with... although they might be transgenic! ☺ That means more and more people have made theirs Hippocrates' famous phrase: *Let food be thy medicine and medicine be thy food.*

---

[6] GMO: Genetically Modified Organism.

## Some distinctions with Jamie in the kitchen

– This smoothie is awesome! It would be great to write down the different mixtures, so we know which ones are the nicest ones.
– Sure! Get a notebook and a pen.
– Yeah... Well...
– I know. Writing things down is tiring, isn't it?
– Pss.
– Maybe you could record short videos. What about that?
– Sounds good to me.
– I'm so glad to see that you're into smoothies now. God bless the day that I took you to *Life Mastery*[7].
– I know. Before I attended, just looking at a lettuce made me puke.
– And now, here you are, juicing grass!

---

[7] *Life Mastery*: one of Tony Robbins' seminars. Its main focus is health in all areas: physical, emotional, metal, in relationships.

— It's wheat grass.
— Yeah. Fine. Chlorophyll.
— It's easier to drink when you add water to it.
— But what about the super model figure you have now? And how strong you are? And all the energy you've got? Eh?
— I'd need to punch a couple of extra holes onto my belt. And, look, I've had these jeans for a couple of years now, since I was 13, and I could hardly button them up back then. And, you see? I can fit a fist in their waist now!
— It was only 4 months ago that we attended UPW[8] and when Joseph[9] told us about not eating meat, you came into a shock!
— Only 4 months ago?
— Yes! Not only meat, remember? Dairy, sugar, gluten, fried things, eggs, sea food. Not all banned, of course, but reduce the

---

[8] *UPW, Unleash the Power Within*: one of Tony Robbins' seminars. It's about discovering our boundless potential and rewrite our story.
[9] Joseph McClendon III

consumption... nearly to 0%.

— What did they say about chicken?

— The said that when they slaughtered them, if the blood was not removed, their meat got full of urine and that's why people eating a lot of poultry could have gout, which is caused by uric acid, which is present in piss.

— But, wasn't that with red meat?

— Yes! You're right! I mixed them. The chickens' thing was they washed them in the water that had also the contents of their cloacae, which is the place birds have for eggs, piss and poop.

— That's right: they washed the chickens in the water containing their pee and shit. I hadn't eaten chicken ever since. That was easy.

— I remember how you said, in one of the breaks, how you didn't know what to eat, that it was impossible to eat if anything if you remove all the list they had just given us.

— Yes, I know. And you told me I could eat the same things you ate.

— Exactly. And you answered to me that was very boring, all greens and fruit and nuts.

— Amazing.

— ...

— When we left the course, you had decided to go through the challenge of eating healthily for 9 days. The resolution lasted...

— One day!

— That was funny. You spent the whole day fasting and, for dinner,

you had a huge steak with French fries!
— It was delicious. The best ever.
— I thought *Life Mastery* could have been difficult for you. But you went through it all.
— Well; that thing that tasted of garlic nearly made me throw up and I just couldn't take it on day 2.
— So? I found the wrap up of a muffin in the lady's toilette. And those facilities were only used by the seminar's attendees.
— Really?
— Really. And there you are, tough man, you didn't succumb to temptation and on day 5 you started eating lettuce and salads, something I had never seen you do ever before.
— Salads are still a bit of an effort for me, but I love fruit and nuts. You know what I saw in YouTube? I saw a video where they said the man acting as Thor in *The Avengers* is vegan.
— Wow! Look at that!
— And I've also learned a recipe with banana, vanilla, cinnamon and almond milk that you put on a toast. Do we try it?
— Sure! We have all the ingredients.
— Almond milk... It's so tasty! I love it!
— I asked you to try it some months ago, or a year ago, and you told me it was disgusting, too sweet.
— I know. I like it now.
— What else do you like now better?
— Dark chocolate. I could never stand it, because I find it too

dark and bitter. Now, I love it. Over all, if it comes with almonds or hazelnuts.

— I think that's a sign of you getting alkaline.

— Like bleach?

— The very same!

— ...

— Come on, boy! It's only a joke! Well, actually, it's a bit the same, as the pH of bleach is high and you getting alkalised I mean your pH would be higher. At least, that's what many say.

— That's what they said in the course.

— Our bodies know what they need. When we feed them with a lot of carbohydrates and sugars and stuff that's not nourishing, we tend to eat more and more, because the very reason there's no nourishment and the body seeks for more. If we are into the habit of eating a lot of sugars, and buns, and bread, and biscuits, the more we eat to placate the hunger and the fatter we get but remain not well nourished because these things lack many of the ingredients we need.

— I see.

— Remember those times when we went hiking you kept drinking *Aquarius*? Sugarless soft drinks contain artificial sweeteners, and the effect these have is that the more we drink, the more we need to drink. They make us thirstier.

— Why is that?

— Well. I don't know if this side effect of the sweeteners is intended or not, meaning, the more people drink, the more product they sell, the more money they make.

— Really?

— I'm just telling you the facts. Another fact is that once you went back to plain water or water with a bit of lemon, you were not that thirsty.

— And my mouth was not so sticky.

— And you know what they also say in courses: "Don't believe anything, you try it yourself and see if it works for you".

— So are we going to measure our pH to see if it's high?

— If you want, we can measure it in your urine. But, what for? You feel stronger, you've lost weight, you can walk faster, sleep less time and you're not tired, your skin looks brilliant, you have less acne now and you even smell better. And I'm pretty sure your bowel works better too. What more of a proof do you want?

— So you're telling me all this is because I'm eating fruits and veggies and nuts and seeds and smoothies and nearly no meat and all those other things? Also, my pee is nearly colourless, by the way.

— Love, I can't assure you a hundred per cent how much of it would be placebo and how much would be pure biochemistry. Now, you're very conscious of what you eat and of looking after your health; you didn't before; at least, not so much. Plus you're exercising too. Everything adds up.

— Ok.

— By walking on fire, you learned you could do anything you'd put your mind to, even though it were something everybody else would

say it's impossible.
— That was a bit too much. I was really scared.
— So was I, what do you think? But, scared and all, we walked on fire.
— Are you positive it was hot? I can't believe it, because I didn't feel the heat at all.
— More than 200°C, that's for sure.
— Fuck! Oops! Sorry...
— Have you set any goal you thought before that it would be impossible to achieve?
— Eat veggies!
— Congratulations!
— It's so much better to eat this way! I don't know why everybody just don't do it.
— Because changing habits requires an effort, even though they bring us a better good. You know this already: we feel sure in our comfort zone, although this comfort zone is not that good. What's outside this zone is unknown and we found it scary and fear makes us feel uncomfortable.
— But it's so much better to eat like we do! I don't miss meat. Well, cheese and bacon sandwiches... I do. But I eat one some Fridays. They're so tasty!
— Honey, you witnessed my eating habits for a long while, you attended UPW and you had to go through *Life Mastery* to make it yours and decide to change. It took you one second to make the shift: once you decided it, that was it. There was a turning point

for you where you said to yourself 'that's it, I'm committed to my health now'.

— True.

— I think it was very powerful when you stood up in front of everybody and, microphone in hand, committed to take the responsibility of your own health, and how you'd be around friends with the same interest in health. That's extremely powerful.

— Why?

— First, by saying out loud, microphone or not microphone, what you're committed to do in a total state of conviction is like a decree: you decree something and anything different simple won't be acceptable. Second, by surrounding yourself with peers with the same standards, you hold one another accountable. It's easy to stick to some expansion of the comfort zone if more of us are on the same boat.

– Makes sense. My friends have seen the changes in me and now they are eating different now and doing more exercise.

– You're making the world a better place! Ripple effect. You are influencing others by example.

– I'm thinking now of that movie you showed us one day, the movie of that guy who ate in McDonald's for a month

– *Super Size me.*

– Yeah! That guy got fat indeed!

– Not only that. During the month that he was going through this 'diet', he went through thorough regular medical examinations. More than once, the doctors heavily advise he left the experiment because his health was degrading so rapidly there could be a possibility of reaching a point of no return. I remember his liver was very badly affected and something that could make you think twice before you eat junk food again: his sexual desire and capability to perform went down to nearly nothing. His girlfriend was not impressed at all!

– Mum!

– I know, I know. Too much information. Just do me a favour and keep it in mind for when the time comes.

– Ok.

– If I remember well, it took him around 2 years to go back to the levels where he was before shooting the documentary.

— 2 years!

— Plus his girlfriend was a dietitian!

— Mario and I never went back to a McDonalds after that. Well, we did, but we only ate fries.

— Before the movie, I never thought that food could be so damaging for the health.

— Me either. But, is it really that bad? Don't you think people could exaggerate about the alkaline stuff?

— To be honest, I've read and heard both sides: people recovering from cancer due to a change in their diets —among them, two friends of mine—, and others posting here and there that even though they had changed their diets, or their beloved ones, they still died. But, you see, we don't know the whole stories.

— Mmm.

— However, it's pretty obvious that processed food, full of oil and fat and sugars and sweeteners can't be as good for your body as natural foods. One question: how do you feel after Christmas lunch?

— Stuffed, tired, with low energy, my breath smells worse the following day, and my sweat, and my pee is darker and I don't always go to the toilette the next day.

— See? Simple as. Just common sense.

— I see.

— And when we feed animals with non-natural stuff, they get sick.

— I've heard dogs can die if they're fed with chocolate.
— I think that's when chocolate contains a chemical called theobromine. Their bodies can't process this substance very well and it can cause death from heart palpitations, seizures and cardiac/respiratory arrest.
— You sound like a doctor now!
— I had a subject on food science a looong time ago.
— So they can have like attacks?
— Pretty much. You know what's very interesting?
— What?
— These are the same symptoms us humans get when we drink caffeine!
— Really?
— Yeap!
— Interesting. So you die if you drink coffee?
— A human needs to take a lot more coffee to die than a dog needs to eat chocolate to die. As for the symptoms, there they are. Did you realise there are a lot of people who say that until they have a coffee in the morning they are worthless? They get the extra kick of energy from the caffeine, and that's depleting their energy in the long term.
— Good I don't like coffee.
— I love the smell, but not the taste. I'm glad, because I grew up in an environment when drinking coffee would be sort of an initiation rite, kind of children don't drink coffee, adults do.

— Mmm.

— Another thing. I'm thinking about the serrano ham and Iberian ham.

— Yummie!

— The difference in the price is huge, but so is in the taste and the properties.

— Iberian is so tasty! And it melts in your mouth!

— Iberian ham comes from pigs that are mainly fed with acorn and they live freely. Their fat melts at the same temperature of our bodies is, so it's true it melts in your mouth. The chemical composition of their fat is what it is because of what they eat.

— So 'it melts in your mouth' is not only a way of speaking!

— There's science behind it, you see? So it's pretty clear to me that our own bodies won't be the same if we eat one thing or another, because, chemically, there are differences.

— Do you mean our meat and fat are different depending on what we eat? Like pigs'?

— Of course? I haven't sliced anybody to take a look, of course, but you can tell the effects of the different diets in the weight, the skin, the hair, the smell, the agility and flexibility, the energy levels, diseases...

— Ok.

— Think of my friends rather than yours. Your friends are young. Think of those friends my age that have been on poor diets for a long time and how you yourself are amazed by the fact they're my age.

— True!
— However…
— Of course there's a however!
— However, it's not all down to what we eat. Our thoughts change our biochemistry, as you well know by now. So it's not only what you eat, it's the state you're in when you're eating and digesting.
— Not good to have a French class after lunch…
— Nice try!
As for thoughts, you can change your interpretation of the events around you.
— How do you do that?
— I think the easiest is that, when you're eating, you're focused on what you're eating: feel the flavour, the texture, the temperature; feel grateful for the food and imagine how it is nourishing your body.
— So… no watching videos while eating.
— What do you think?
— Maybe I can do both things at the same time?
— Up to you, love…
— Ok. What if we prepare a smoothie with almond milk, apricot and banana?
— What if avocado or blueberries instead of banana?
— Sure. I'll peel the apricots.
— I'll prepare the avocado.
— Thank you so much!

— Thank you, sweetheart. I love cooking with you. Because this is cooking, right?
— Oh, well. For you... I'm guessing this is cooking alright.
— One day, I'll learn how to boil potatoes, to start with, and you'll see!
— Yeah, sure. We'll see...

## 8. STAR WARS

# "Our Greatest Fear"

Our greatest fear is not that we are inadequate,
but that we are powerful beyond measure.

It is our light, not our darkness, that frightens us.
We ask ourselves, Who am I to be brilliant,
gorgeous, handsome, talented and fabulous?

Actually, who are you not to be?
You are a child of God.

Your playing small does not serve the world.
There is nothing enlightened about shrinking
so that other people won't feel insecure around you.

We were born to make manifest the glory of God within us.
It is not just in some; it is in everyone.

And, as we let our own light shine, we consciously give
other people permission to do the same.
As we are liberated from our fear,
our presence automatically liberates others.

Author: Marianne Williamson

They say Nelson Mandela read these words when he was pronounced President of South Africa. Others say he didn't.

Anyway, the first time I read them I felt like saying "take this chalice away from me". I used to be scared of my inner power. Things are different now.

> *I now choose to embrace my inner power. I now choose to create the space for this inner power of mine so it can surge in all its glory. I envision my power flowing outwards, no matter what the rest of the world says. I am pure energy and I know anything I wish for can be manifested, limitlessly. I listen to my heart, which is god's voice, and completely trust its voice. I experience where desire, which is divinely inspired, can take me to. I witness what magnificent things I can make happen and how they improve the lives of many. I bring heaven to earth. I am a prophet that walks the talk. I am a model of how much we can achieve if we free our minds and let ourselves be guided by our hearts and spirit, by love, by our divine nature. In the moments when my mind plays tricks on me, I get stressed and thus less resourceful, I will accept it and will go back to the love track, for I know there's an unlimited support for me out there. I am the creator of the magnificent, fulfilling outstanding life I deserve.*

How do you think your days would be if you start them with words along these lines? Do you think it would make any difference?

Think for a second: How much has your life changed in the last year? In the last 5 years? Have you accomplished your goals? Are you any nearer to them? What are you doing differently? What are you learnings? Do you sit down and complain or do you do anything about it? In 10 years, what will you regret? What would you do differently if you were to die next year?

I suggest you take a pen and paper, or a keyboard and a screen, and answer all these questions and any others you've been postponing to think about or you just expect life to get them sorted out for you... miraculously. Then, move your ass; life is short, far too short and it's only up to you to make the most of it.

Reminder: you're the only one responsible for your life. Also remember things are just facts: it's all about how we decide to read them, as if curses or as if gifts.

## (Mario and I) a long time ago in a galaxy far, far away

— What is it? Are you alright?

— I am, sweet, I am. I was just thinking.

— What were you thinking?

— I was thinking how my fearful thoughts make me feel low, with no strength, little energy. Although I know that fear is just in my head, because I'm scared of things that haven't happened yet. It's a bit like that exercise we did in one of the seminars we went to, remember? I think it was 'put your arm up tomorrow'. It doesn't make any sense! Same as worrying about things that are not there yet. There's another exercise for this: think of a lemon, imagine its smell and texture, grab a knife, cut a slice, put it in your mouth and your mouth starts to salivate. There's no lemon, but your mouth waters anyway.

— Gross! But if I think of having a motorbike that is not the same as having one.

— Sure. But if you close your eyes and imagine what it is like to drive a motorbike, you feel the wind on you face, the vibration of the engine all over your body and you see the road in front of you, your body will produce the molecules that you'd be producing if you were actually having the experience. Your biochemistry changes.
— I see. I don't know. I don't think it's the same thing going to a party or thinking about one.
— I guess it's a matter of how vividly you can imagine things. I'm not there yet either, honey. Maybe you can just think a party can go great or not so great and that's probably what your experience will be, but with your mind's eye, you can make as good as you like!
— Ah.
— I've listened and read interviews to people who had been able to survive under extreme conditions thanks to the discipline in their thinking behaviour. For instance, Nelson Mandela. Do you remember that movie we watched about him, Clint Eastwood's?
— Which one?
— That black man who had been in prison for 27 years and the movie starts when he's the president of his country and doesn't fire anyone, he just wants peace and harmony. South Africa was divided both economically and in blacks and whites. I think Mandela's point was to get his countrymen closer together through sports, and they put all their energy and focus on winning the rugby World Cup sometime in the 90's. I'm guessing 95, as he was elected president in 94. The rugby World Cup was taking place in South Africa and they won the final, remember this?

— So it was all true? I thought it was a movie.

— True story. Can you imagine 27 years in prison for no reason and not going crazy, for starters? Or going violent? Or just perish for the whole nonsense of it all? But as he got out of jail, he said he forgave the people who put him there and he was later on elected president. From this position, he could have easily taken revenge of them, but he chose to lead on the basis of love and harmony and the *we-are-all-one* ideal.

— Wow.

— Yes. Wow! What an example!

— He could have chosen to think what bastards they've been, putting me in jail no reason, what a huge injustice, how life is a bitch and a bull shit and plan revenge on the way out. But he didn't.

— Hmm.

— Do you remember how you felt when we were on our way to walk on fire?

— I was so scared!

— What I saw from the outside was that you were very pale, your hands were sweaty and cold, you didn't walk in a straight line, your phrases were not always complete or made sense, you were swallowing frequently, or you tried to. Most likely, your mouth was dry.

— Really? I can't remember. I just remember I was scared.

— It was the thoughts you were having then that made you sweat, your mouth dry and the rest of the things. Notice all you were actually doing was walking. Just walking! I know, barefoot, but

you were just walking. Everything else was in your head. The only difference between you at that moment and you one hour before were your thoughts.
— My thoughts were I could get burned!

— You were scared of the future. About something you considered that could be hurtful in the future. It was something that was not actually happening to you during those moments.
— Wow! That's true!
— And that's with you knowing it was not obligatory at all, that you could choose whether to walk on fire or not, that it was only up to you to decide.
— But I did want to do it.
— I know. But no-one was forcing you to do so.

— Everyone was doing it.

— We can't know that for sure. Maybe someone backed out. We do know, however, that thousands walked the fire. Again, it was voluntary; what most do should not dictate what we decide to do. At least, that's what I do; otherwise, we would all be exactly the same! All white sheep!

— I watched a documentary in YouTube and they said sheep distinguish one another by their faces. They all look the same to me, but they can tell each other apart. And that's with those weird eyes they've got, with the black part like the hole of a piggy bank.

— Odd! Thank you. Sheep normally form herds; they find safety in numbers. If the wolf comes around for a feast, a sheep going solo would be easy-peasy for the wolf, but if there are many sheep, he could only eat one or two and the rest would all survive.

— Why do you always say sheep and not zebras, for example?

— I guess it's because we can easily see sheep around, but not that many zebras.

— Pity. They're so cute!

— It's all about the money, sweet. Sheep are more productive than sheep moneywise.

— It could be cows instead of sheep. There are cows all over too.

— Good observation. Maybe sheep are more common in proverbs because within their herd, they are very much alike than cows. Humans, collectively, also feel safer in groups with similarities. That's the reason why, quite often, we refrain from doing things

different to what our group does and when we decide to do something different, the rest of the group will do whatever it takes to bring the lost sheep back to the herd, in the name of safety. The weak succumb and they surrender to the power of the group, to what they imagine to be safer.
— I'm... a bit lost.
— Ok. An example. Think of school. At lunch time, they give you, let's say, salad, fish and an apple. You love apples and you love eating them between meals, rather than as dessert. You next prefer time to eat them would be before the salad and the fish.
— Right.
— All the group, all your class mates, would normally eat their apples after the salad and the fish. That would be the rule for the group. You come along and eat your apple for starters. What do you think the other children's reaction would be?
— Some would probably me ask why am I eating the apple before the salad and the fish.
— What would you do?
— Tell them I feel like it.
— Right. Now, another child says to you that eating the apple first is wrong, that you are supposed to eat it at the end.
— Why would they say that?
— Because they would feel safer if things remained the same. Also be because they would have loved to eat the apple first but they're scared and they dislike the fact you're doing it and they aren't.
— But they can do it if they like?

— They believe it would be bad for their digestion if they ate the apple first. They are scared they might have a stomach ache if they eat it first.

— Do apples give you belly ache if you eat them before lunch?

— Most likely, only if you believe they'd do so. Do you remember what I told you about not believing anything they'd say to you, that it was for you to experience it and then decide what was your truth?

— Yeah, I do remember. I wouldn't think an apple would hurt eating it one time or another.

— Cool. So, would you still eat the apple before lunch, regardless what the other children say?

— Sure!

— Think of a child in your class that is quite or shy.

— Alex.

— What do you think Alex would do if he were to eat an apple before lunch and someone said to him that it could make him be sick?

— Probably, he wouldn't eat it.

— That's going back to the herd, to be just like all the other sheep. Do you see it now?

— Ah! I do!

— I'm glad I made it clearer for you, love.

— Thank you, mamasita.

— My pleasure.

— Mom: the other day, I saw a video in YouTube. It was a girl who

wanted to be a gymnast, and she didn't have legs. No legs! And she won a lot of medals and now she's doing something and she's teaching other people. Hallucinating!
— Do you think she was ever told what a silly thing, being a gymnast with no legs, are you stupid or what?
— Her mom was in the video and she said they grew her never saying to her she couldn't do something. And she was in the video playing baseball and basketball. A-mazing, dude!
— She saw herself as a sheep of a different colour and didn't pay attention to those saying to her: 'where do you think you're going, smart ass? Gymnast with no legs? You're an idiot!' Her mother helped her big time to grow self-confidence, but no doubt not everybody along the way was the same.
— It's like *Babe*, the pig. He wanted to be a shepherd for the sheep, that were stupid, and the farmer took him to the contest for shepherd dogs, and the other farmers laughed at them and Babe won.
— Exactly. And that gymnast girl, do you think she looked happy in the video?
— Sure. And she has a car and she lives by herself.
— What's all this teaching you?
— ...that I can do or be whatever I want?
— Of course! Always in a harmonious way, right? Do you realise the girl had her mother by her side and Babe had the farmer by its side? The mother and the farmer were their support.
— Ok.

— Quite often, the support we need is not so close by, but there are always resources out there, even though we don't even know where or who or what they could be. The first step is sometimes get a new set of friends, to surround yourself with people you admire, that would inspire you, models of the person you wish to become.
— So?
— You can also read books of those who've achieved something extraordinary. Listen to them. Imitate them. Of course they're also human and they can put the foot in it, but if they screwed it, they just say they've learned how not to do it and try a different approach. Many of this very successful people share their experience with generosity, they share with us what they've done differently and let us know where they made mistakes so we can learn from them and move faster.
— Are there videos in YouTube too?
— Lots. I can tell you names of those I think they're funnier, if you like, because you can laugh and learn at the same time.
— CooOool!
— Now that we're talking about this, there's a book I'd love to tell you about with a lot more detail.
— ...
— It's called *Power versus Force*. I learned so much from it! And I'm sure you can relate to it because you've seen a lot of the concepts in the *Star Wars* movies.
— Is it ok if we talk about it another day?
— Of course, love! I know you have an important match on line in a

few minutes.
- Yep! Thank you, mamasita!
- Love you.
- Love you too.
- Love you three.

Nelson Mandela
1918-2013 [10]

*Thank you, Nelson, for showing me what life is all about.*

---

[10] This photograph is Apple's property and a tribute to Nelson Mandela.

# 9. MONEY

The three most influential groups in my early days on this planet were: family, religion and school.

Allow me, please, to briefly share with you the ideas that these statements wired my brain with regarding money.

By birth, I belong to the working class. Traditionally, this class belief system includes pearls such as: the rich take advantage of the poor, rich people are mean, they think they're superior to the rest of the world and the like. You get the idea.

The way to make money in this statement would be working, preferably as an employee. "There's no shame in hard work" would quite often turn into a great excuse to set for a mediocre job for life.

In conclusion: if being rich meant compromising righteousness and high standard ethics could cover for a low profile job plus we add the peer pressure of belonging to the herd... what do you get? A screwed up brain that would have to get a lot of work done on it in order to overcome all this programming and be able to think outside the box.

As for Catholicism, being rich is a sin. And sin, if a big one, sends sinners straight to hell. Wow! That's major! Hell is forever! Better to remain poor. The "earn our bread with the sweat of our brow", tattooed in the heart and soul of many, stated it very clearly: the way to make ends meet is to work hard. Folks: nothing like a free and biased interpretation of a book trimmed here and there over centuries to change the life style of a few billion people in the planet!

When I was a student, it was quite frequent that students not precisely brilliant would end up teaching young children. The teacher degree was easier to get than other university courses. As for secondary education, many university students of assorted degrees chose this path of teaching either because they couldn't find a job in the corporate world or because they loved enjoying the same long holidays and privileges of a schedule tailored for children.

Of course there are fantastic, inspirational, devoted teachers; I'm just sharing my personal experience.

As a result, those teachers in charge of modelling our young brains and spirits ended up being not the smartest tools in the tool box or rejections from other arenas. Not only that, in many cases they happened to be badly paid employees under crappy contracts, with little or no security of where they would be the coming year. What could these poor guys teach us about finances? ¡Nada! Nothing at all! Would they know anything about concepts such as 'financial literacy', 'financial freedom'? To put in statistical terms: if a teacher knows the true meaning behind these terms, that would be considered an outlier, i.e., one black sheep out of a million white sheep: negligible.

To make it even more fun, to the mixture above add up the 'you are worthy of what you have', the fact that wages are taboo —even for those who wouldn't hesitate providing full details of any of their physiological functions, including those enjoyed in company of others—, the unwritten law of not ever hold conversations about money and... *voilà!* The cocktail is served.

Nearly every book addressing financial education includes these depressing statistics: at 65 years of age, 95% of the population are either dead or dead broke.

However, what happens with the other 5%? Easy: they know something the other 95% doesn't!

The next question would be: can the 95% learn what the 5% knows? Yes, under one condition: that the poor start thinking like the rich; everything starts by deleting all those beliefs that keep the 95% where they are and by acquiring the habits the 5% practice and the beliefs this 5% has. Easy peasy.

## Mario and I, on a Saturday morning, first day of the month

— Who's helping me with the money this month?

— Me! Me!

— Great! Here's The Envelope.

— Is this the money you've made this month?

— I made some more, but this is the part I'm going to use for the splits.

— Okey dokey!

— Do we make a start? Would you like to count it?

— Yep! That's the coolest part.

— ...

— ... nine hundred, one thousand and... twenty... four.

— Right. Keep the thousand and leave the 24 in The Envelope for next month.

— Yes, mama!

— Right. So let's split the notes: household, investing, holidays, the

new car, education, blow money and tithing.
— How much here?
— For investing and education, 10%, so $100 in each envelope.
— ...90 and 100. Done. Next!
— For the new car and holidays, 5% each, so two fifties.
— Done! What else?
— To blow and tithing, 7.5%, so $75 each.

— What was tithing again?
— To give away.
— Are you going to give all that away?
— Yes.
— That much??
— You see? At the beginning, I found it hard to give this tithing money away, but I understood that was the only way to change.
— Change what?
— To change my old story: that feeling that I never had enough, so

I needed to keep it all. By doing the exercise of giving away to someone I feel like giving it to, or an institution, I feel extremely fulfilled inside, I understand that I have more than enough for myself and for you and those receiving it are delighted, so I make the light and energy circulate.

— Like when you gave the old car to your friend?

— Exactly.

— What will we be doing with the blow money this month?

— I'll treat myself to a massage and we can go together to the new spa, does it sound good to you?

— Dunno. What do you do in a spa?

— It's an indoor water circuit, with lots of different pools: with water jets, bubble baths, saunas, hot water, cold water…

— Ok-k! But not on Sunday, because there's a Formula 1 car race.

— *Kein Problem!* The weekend after.

— What else?

— The rest, for the household: food, fuel, clothes we need… and I'll be separating $80 for emergencies.

— Like what?

— Like the washing machine breaking down.

— I see.

— Now, let's count and see how much we have in the Investing envelope, ok?

— I count.

—… eight hundred and seventy eight and… why do you have coins in this envelope?

— Because I put something every day, even though it's only a few cents. This is the envelope for our financial freedom.

— Do you send it all to the stock market?

— Sure. I follow the plan I showed you. Do you remember what it was like?

— Yeah. And are you making all the money you planned to make?

— Well... I was very much ahead of my plan but I became a bit greedy, I entered into too many oil positions and now it's going to take me a few months to recover, but I'll go back to where I was and, son, I've learned an extremely valuable lesson: put the eggs in more baskets! It's called asset allocation.

— Oh.

— My shares have also gone down a lot, but they'll go back up; that's the nature of the market. As we have bought stock of very sound companies, it's just a matter of time that they go back up.

— It's a bit boring now.

— I agree. But, as you know, 'the more patient you are, the more money you'll make'.

— And did you have stock when you were a girl?

— With the little money I made as presents when I received my first communion, and taking advice from my mother, I bought some stock of the only one telephone company back then.

— Does granny know about the stock market?

— Not really. Just like 95% of the people in the world, by the way!

— So what happened next?

— I went to the bank and they bought the shares for me. I never studied the company or the graph.

— Never??

— No, son. I never did. I know it sounds outrageous to you, because you took this course at 11 (at 11!). If I recall well, they never mentioned in that course that 90% of the investors in the stock market do not follow any system; they choose the companies to invest in because they sound familiar, or based on what the media says or because of what a brother in law tells them, in the line of "huge potential, I wish I had the money, don't let this opportunity escape".

— Really? What a silly thing to do.

— You smart ass! But, honey, only 3 years ago, I was clueless about the stock market.

— No clue at all? *Nada?*

— Nothing, love. No-thing-at-all. The concept of 'share' was a bit of a blur for me, let alone 'option'.

— Holly Moly!

— You'd be surprised how many other thing people don't know and you do know.

— Like what?

— For instance, the concept that money should be working for you instead of or as well as you for the money. See? It took me 20 years, 20 years! to figure out I didn't want to sell my life anymore, that I was done with working the amount of hours another person imposed on me and that doing what they wanted me to do. Again... 20 solid years!

— Wow! That's quite some time, mum...

— I know! Better late than ever, though! Plus I'm passing my experience onto you, so it's not all wasted.

— What else people don't know?

— The power of the compound interest.

— But we do that in school. That's easy.

— The theory might be easy, but the implications of it are something different. And only a few apply the knowledge. You see? The trick is to be disciplined enough as to take apart some money every single month, at least; even though is as little as $100 per month. And then, invest that money in the stock market. When you put together the increase in the price of the stock and the power of the compound interest, after some years, it's a huge amount of money.

— Yeah, I remember the spreadsheet you showed me. And they don't know that?

— At least, they don't apply it. Many think you need a lot of money to invest in the stock market. And that's ignorance, because it's not true.

— What else?

— Do you know what self-sabotage is?

— It rings a bell... Like telling yourself lies?

— More or less. Some people are scared of becoming successful, even though they think it's the other way around. And then, when thing start going well, they would find a way to stop the process and screw it all so they don't become successful.

— Whaaaat? They don't want to have money?

— I know it may sound strange, to put it lightly, but, you know, some parents are talking all the time about how mean or dishonest the rich are so when their children grow up, they don't want to have money because they think their parents would think badly of them, like they're mean and dishonest.

— That's weird...

— I know! But, not only that, as grown-ups we don't even realise we think that way because we've heard them so many times we think they're true. So, honey: don't believe a word anyone tells you! At least, question it all and experience it all before you take a decision of whether something is true or not.

— Cool it, mama. I will!

— I learned a lot about these things in a book called *Secrets of a Millionaire Mind*. But I think you don't need to read it, because you know you can get whatever you put your mind to, you already have a plan to make your money work for you and you already know what you'll be doing when you grow up.

— Do I? I can't remember...

— You told me you'd do whatever you'd like doing, that you'd be the best at it and that you'd share it with others. I must say I helped you a bit with this...

— Yeah. I do remember now. But I still don't know what I'll be doing.

— Don't worry. You'll figure that out later.
— Ok.
— At this stage, you know some of my new friends and how they're working on projects that make them very happy. You also know people that work for a salary and how much they complain, at least, some of them. So, having a job was something you had ruled out, at least, for the moment. But feel free to try. Whatever you want.
— Yeah. Those friends of yours have a lot of fun, I think. But they work a lot, they say.
— Do you think it's worth it for them?
— I think so, because they travel a lot and have a great time.
— Let's see what else I can tell you.
— Where are we going to go on holidays with the money in the holidays' envelope?
— Last year we used it to go London, just you and I. Remember? It took us a while to put the money together, but it was so worth it! We had such a good time! We saw so many things, and visited many too. I had visited London a few times before, but I had never gone to touristy places, because in many of them you have to pay a ticket to have access to them and I felt guilty and I always travelled trying to spend as little as possible. Now, I don't anymore, because the money we used was already assigned for the trip.
— The best were the spare ribs with barbeque sauce.
— What about *The Phantom of the Opera?*

— That was cool too!

— I think you were not that cool about it. I'm guessing when I gave you the envelope with the ticket, you thought something like 'What the hell is my mother taking me to tonight? I'll be so tired in the evening, after walking around London for the whole day! I'd rather go to the park and feed the squirrels'.

— Pss... But I liked it a lot.

— I know! You didn't even blinked during the show. Over all, during the second part.

— So what's the trick?

— With what?

— With putting money aside to go on holidays.

— Yeah. I've just hinted to it. You see? For me, enjoying things that I always considered luxurious is pretty new. I always thought that was an unnecessary expense and spending money on them felt me feel so guilty I hardly ever allowed myself to spend the money and enjoy myself. This comes from my childhood; that's what I saw as a kid all the time: saving, saving, saving. That was the thing to do. And you know what?

— What?

— By me thinking that way, saving and saving, that made it impossible to make more money. Why the hell would the universe give me more money if I don't enjoy it and I feel guilty around it? Looking for pleasure and avoiding pain moves us. If money equals suffering, I won't have it, because I'll be avoiding pain.

— Oh.

– In school, the used to tell us that Jesus Christ was poor.
– And he wasn't?
– His father was a carpenter, and 2000 years ago, being a carpenter was like being an architect... a few years ago, meaning, a very lucrative profession. And a very well-considered one, like, high standard. Now, many architects have no jobs, unfortunately.
– I see.
– And the apostles, the men Christ hang around with and taught, they were fishermen. In school, they also told me they were poor. But it seems that, back then, being a fisherman was also a profession that produced a high income.
– Did they tell you lies in school?
– They told me what they had been told. I'm guessing they never questioned the things they were taught. And, you know, it's so common to be sold the rich are bad and the poor and good and a lot happier, they wouldn't doubt Christ was poor.
– Yeah?
– Have you ever seen a good rich person in a movie?
– Let's see. Let me think...
– Think, yeah, go ahead. Keep thinking and let me know, if you find any. I only know of a rich man who was 'good', and I've seen many many movies!
– Who?
– Keep thinking. You've seen the movie I'm thinking of.
– Oh, come on! Don't leave me hanging!

— Later. Be patient. Another question: what do you think, that you can help people more if you have a lot of money or if you have little money?

— A lot! What a silly question.

— I agree with you. And those with enough money so they don't need to work anymore, they also have time to help others. And to have fun too, of course. And, listen to this, fulfilment. That's the key word.

— No job and no school. Sounds like a plan to me!

— Playing video games or computer games or whatever games you play on screens won't make you very happy, although that's what you think now.

— ...

— Yeah. You know it's true. Don't look at me that way!

— Let me think about it...

— You learn fast! Well, love, we're ready for this month. Thanks a million for your help. I so enjoy doing things with you!

— No! Thank you!

— Love you, son.

— Hey! What was the movie with a good rich man in it?

— *Forrest Gump.* He shared his money and did good things for others and they made his character being a 'intelligence challenged" person. So they sold us this mathematical equation: rich + good = stupid.

— Mmm. Makes sense.

Made in the USA
San Bernardino, CA
16 March 2017